T0056589

Grains

Resources Series

Peter Dauvergne & Jane Lister, *Timber*

Michael Nest, *Coltan*

Elizabeth R. DeSombre & J. Samuel Barkin, *Fish*

Jennifer Clapp, *Food, 2nd edition*

David Lewis Feldman, *Water*

Gavin Fridell, *Coffee*

Gavin Bridge & Philippe Le Billon, *Oil*

Derek Hall, *Land*

Ben Richardson, *Sugar*

Ian Smillie, *Diamonds*

Adam Sneyd, *Cotton*

Grains

BILL WINDERS

polity

First published in 2017 by Polity Press

Polity Press
65 Bridge Street
Cambridge CB2 1UR, UK

Polity Press
350 Main Street
Malden, MA 02148, USA

ISBN-13: 978-0-7456-8803-9
ISBN-13: 978-0-7456-8804-6(pb)

A catalogue record for this book is available from the British Library.

Library of Congress Cataloging-in-Publication Data

Names: Winders, William, 1971- author.
Title: Grains / Bill Winders.
Description: Cambridge, UK ; Malden, MA : Polity Press, 2016. | Includes
  bibliographical references and index.
Identifiers: LCCN 2016016764| ISBN 9780745688039 (hardback : alk. paper) |
  ISBN 9780745688046 (pbk.)
Subjects: LCSH: Grain trade--Political aspects. | Agriculture and state. |
  Agriculture and politics. | Food supply--Political aspects. | Geopolitics.
Classification: LCC HD9030.5 .W555 2016 | DDC 338.1/731--dc23 LC record available at
https://lccn.loc.gov/2016016764

Typeset in 10.5 on 13pt Scala by
Servis Filmsetting Ltd, Stockport, Cheshire
Printed and bound in the UK by Clays Ltd, St Ives PLC

For further information on Polity, visit our website:
politybooks.com.

For my mother and father,
Kathleen and David Winders
To whom I do not say "Thank You" enough.

Contents

Figures and Tables   viii
Acknowledgments   x

1   Grains for Food, Grains for Feed   1

2   Grains and the US Food Regime   24

3   The Search for New Markets   52

4   Feed Grains, Food Grains, and World
    Hunger   80

5   Genetically Engineered Grains   107

6   Seeds of Change   135

    Notes   161
    Selected Readings   179
    Index   191

Figures and Tables

Figures

1.1 World Production for Maize, Rice, Soybeans, and Wheat, 1960–2015 11

2.1 World Wheat Production, 1960–2015 33

3.1 European Wheat Production and Exports, 1960–2015 64

3.2 European and US Wheat Exports as a Percent of World Exports, 1960–2015 65

3.3 World Wheat Exports, 1960–2015 66

3.4 Global per Capita Meat Consumption, 1961–2011 74

3.5 World Meat Production, 1960–2015 75

3.6 World Meat Production: Number of Animals Slaughtered, 1961–2013 76

4.1 Wheat Exports from India, 1867–1910 85

4.2 Rice Exports from India and Pakistan, 1960–2015 95

4.3 World Quinoa Production, 1961–2014 99

4.4   Quinoa Prices in Bolivia and Peru,
        1991–2012   100

4.5   Indian Beef Production and Exports,
        1960–2015   102

4.6   Maize and Soybean Production in India,
        1960–2015   104

5.1   Adoption of Genetically Engineered
        Crops in the United States, 1996–2015   113

Tables

1.1   Annual World Production of Grains   3

1.2   The ABCDs of the Global Grain Trade
        in 2013   7

Acknowledgments

I am grateful to a number of people who helped me along the way to completing this project. Many people helped me work out the ideas in this book through numerous discussions and exchanges. A few of my colleagues at Georgia Tech regularly talk with me about this project, offering support and feedback: Dan Amsterdam, Doug Flamming, and Steve Usselman. As always, Rick Rubinson was an important source of insight, suggestions, and encouragement. Elizabeth Ransom helped to get me writing in the early stages of my work on this book. I presented Chapter 4 about the connection between grains and world hunger at the Rural Sociological Society annual meeting in 2015 and got important feedback and support from JoAnne Jaffee, Phil Howard, Doug Constance, Alex McIntosh, among others. Also in 2015, I presented Chapter 3 about grains and economic conflicts at the American Sociological Association annual meeting, and I am particularly grateful for the feedback and encouragement that I received there from Ray Jussaume and Kathleen Schwartzman. At Polity Press, I appreciate the guidance and patience that Louise Knight and Nekane Tanaka Galdos showed me as I worked on this book. I am also grateful for the valuable and insightful comments and suggestions given by two anonymous reviewers. And I appreciate the work that Clare Ansell, Susan Beer, and Jane Fricker did in editing the manuscript.

Finally, I owe a deep debt of gratitude to Amy D'Unger, who bore the brunt of my focus on grains and need to share my ideas and new findings. She read and edited the entire manuscript, encouraged me as I worked on this book, and graciously covered for me around the house when work on this book consumed most of my time. Samuel and Violet understood when I needed some extra time or a bit more quiet to get just a little more writing done. It gives me joy and inspiration to see Sam working so hard on his own writing.

In the end, the responsibility for any errors or omissions belongs solely to me.

CHAPTER ONE

Grains for Food, Grains for Feed

The average supermarket has tens of thousands of items, including fresh fruits and vegetables, bakery items, dairy products, meats, and a wide array of processed foods such as crackers, cookies, condiments, boxed dinners, cereals, sodas, frozen foods, and alcohol. There are so many choices. Behind this diversity of products, however, are grains: barley, buckwheat, maize (corn), millet, oats, quinoa, rice, rye, sorghum, and wheat among others.[1] However, just three grains can be found in almost every grocery store aisle: maize, rice, and wheat. Maize pervades supermarket shelves under a variety of names: corn syrup, high fructose corn syrup, corn starch, decyl glucoside, dextrin, dextrose, ferrous gluconate, lactic acid, maltodextrin, xantham gum, and zein among many others. Wheat can be found in thousands of grocery store items in the form of gluten or starch. Likewise, rice takes the form of rice milk and flour, and different forms of rice can be found in a variety of foods, from baby food to beer. Grains in these and other forms permeate most of the processed foods found in supermarkets. Grains are also fed to animals – particularly, cows, chickens, and pigs – that are slaughtered for meat. In short, grains are ubiquitous in supermarkets, belying the apparent variety of foods, which in some fashion are often either grains entirely or contain grains. Even the typical fast food meal in the US – a burger, French fries, and a soda – has far more grains in it than might be apparent at first: grains are in the bun, obviously, but they are also very likely to be in the burger, soda, and ketchup, as well as the oil used to make the French fries. Put simply, grains are everywhere.[2]

Despite the pervasiveness of grains, we do not often think about their deep, underlying political implications, nor do we generally consider why some grains are more predominant than others. Instead, we tend to reflect on whether the amount and types of grains we eat are healthy for us. Maize is often, but not always, the focal point of such discussions. The various forms of maize that appear in foods, especially corn syrup, are argued to be important contributors to health issues, such as obesity. Some popular diets have centered on "low carb" (i.e., "low grains") foods or even urged avoiding grains altogether. Many processed food labels now tout products as "gluten-free" for customers looking to avoid the protein in wheat, barley, and rye. Other public discussions of grains center on issues related to technology, such as genetically modified grains. Rarely do we move beyond these largely individual concerns, primarily about our health, to reflect on the more complex political and economic implications of grains.

Considering the geopolitics of grains is important, though, because people throughout the world consume grains as a central component of their diets. Grains are, therefore, a central factor in political stability, economic well-being, and even cultural heritage and traditions across the globe. Since grains are a central component of most people's diets, one central issue concerning grains is food security: having enough access to grains to provide an adequately nutritious diet. When access to grains decreases, for example because of rising prices, social and political stability can be undermined as people may begin to question or even challenge their political and economic institutions, which have not provided adequate food. Grain production is so widespread that millions of people engage in it as farmers, which means that grains not only provide food but also serve as an important basis for income as well as economic and social status around the world. And finally, grains and their production permeate life and culture around the world, including through music, art, poetry, holiday celebrations, rituals, and even language. For example, the cultivation of rice plays an important role in Japanese origin myths, and many Mexican cities hold festivals every year to celebrate maize. As the production of or access to grains is disrupted, a nation's social, economic, and political stability can also be undermined. Understanding the geopolitics of grains is, therefore, critically important.[3]

The same three grains that are most prevalent in the supermarket – maize, rice, and wheat – are also the grains of greatest political and economic importance across the globe today. One or some combination of these grains forms the basis of diets in every region of the world. Table 1.1 shows annual world grain production for several grains and conveys clearly the importance of maize, rice, and wheat to global food supply. In 2015, world maize production was 967 million metric tons (MMT), rice was 470 MMT, and wheat was 735 MMT. That same year, the total world production of barley, millet, oats, rye, and sorghum together was 277 MMT. This means that the production of all other grains combined

Table 1.1 Annual World Production of Grains (in million metric tons).							
	Maize	Wheat	Rice	Barley	Sorghum	Millet	Oats	Rye
1990	481	588	351	179	53	29	39	36
2000	591	583	399	133	55	27	25	19
2010	835	649	450	123	61	32	20	11
2015	967	735	470	145	68	30	22	12

Source: Foreign Agricultural Service, USDA, "PS&D Online Database," available at http://apps.fas.usda.gov/psdonline/.

totaled only 59 percent of rice production, 38 percent of wheat production, and a mere 29 percent of maize production. Put another way, of the eight grains considered in Table 1.1, maize, rice, and wheat account for almost 90 percent of world grain production. In considering the geopolitics of grains, then, we must focus to a greater extent on the influence of these three grains.[4]

Table 1.1 also shows the recent trends in production, further demonstrating the importance of these grains. Maize production has shown the greatest increase over the past 25 years, doubling from 481 MMT in 1990 to 967 MMT in 2015. While rice and wheat did not match maize's increase over this period, they nonetheless showed substantial growth in production: rice increased by 34 percent and wheat increased by 25 percent. None of the other grains matched this. World production of barley, oats, and rye decreased over this same 25-year period by a combined 75 MMT, or about 29 percent across these three grains. World millet production remained roughly unchanged. World sorghum production increased by 28 percent, but its total increase in production was only 15 MMT, which pales in comparison to the increases of more than 100 MMT for maize, rice, and wheat. Finally, it is also noteworthy that maize, rice, and wheat accounted for 81 percent of world grain production in 1990, but by 2015 these three grains accounted for almost 90 percent of world production. Thus, maize, rice, and wheat dominate world grain production, and this dominance has grown over the past 25 years.

These trends raise two important questions. First, why are maize, rice, and wheat so predominant among world grains? Second, why did the production of these three grains increase so substantially over the past 25 years? We will return to each of these questions, particularly the second one, as they go to the heart of issues examined throughout this book: shifts in the global food system, economic competition and conflicts between grains, world hunger, the use of biotechnology in grain production, and access to land. But for now, our focus is the influence these three grains have on societies.

The distant and recent histories of maize, rice, and wheat reveal their importance not only in terms of feeding populations but also in their political, economic, and social influence. Each of these grains has shaped in various ways the political struggles and economic development of many nations. For example, the land tenure systems (i.e., the ways that landownership is organized) that have arisen around grain production have been linked to the economic and political structures found in societies. Some land tenure systems have been more favorable to the rise of political democracy, while other land tenure systems have inhibited democratic developments and contributed to dictatorships. Sharp reductions in people's access to these grains – which, again, are the basis of most diets around the world – can contribute to food riots and political instability. Economic competition between producers of different grains – or producers of the same grain in different countries – has led to trade wars and increased political tensions. Finally, large companies dominate the grain trade, seed industry, and processing of these grains. This market dominance often translates into significant influence over political institutions and the production and dietary trends in countries around the globe, as well as the exploitation of labor. Through these and other ways, these three grains have shaped the political, economic, and social histories of nations around the world.[5]

The social and political influence of these grains is evident in recent global food crises. World grain prices reached historic heights in 2008, with wheat more than 200 percent higher and rice more than 250 percent higher than 2004–5 levels. The price of maize saw similar though less dramatic increases as well, as did prices for meat and dairy products, for which maize is the main source of feed. This rise in prices made food less accessible for millions of people and world hunger increased. As food prices rose and the threat of hunger spread, more than 30 countries were struck by mass protests and riots. These protests contributed to political instability in a number of countries. In Mexico, tens of thousands of people joined "tortilla protests" in response to the sharp increase in maize prices. In Haiti, the prime minister was removed after a week of food riots in April 2008. Later in 2010, rising grain prices again played a role in protests in Tunisia and Algeria, which then spread across the Middle East as the Arab Spring shook the region. High food prices, particularly for grains, fueled food riots and general protests across the globe that ultimately contributed to violent confrontations and even to changes in political regimes. Grains have the power to transform societies.[6]

Even outside of periods of crisis and change, the political economic influence of grains is apparent. For example, wheat farmers in the US and Europe, rice farmers in Japan and South Korea, and other grain farmers around the world have exerted significant influence over their respective nations' trade and other national policies. Organizations representing maize farmers in the US were strong advocates of expanding trade with Mexico, China, and Cuba in the 1990s and 2000s. Rice farmers in Japan were important advocates of protectionism in the mid-twentieth century. Grain farmers in a variety of nations have influenced a whole range of policies from fiscal and banking policies to labor and social welfare policies.

Grain companies also have a long history of exerting political and economic influence. For many decades, for example, four companies have dominated the global trade in grains: Archer Daniels Midland (ADM), Bunge, Cargill, and Louis Dreyfus. These four agricultural trading firms are referred to as the "ABCDs," and their histories reach back to the 1800s or early

Table 1.2 The ABCDs of the Global Grain Trade in 2013.

Company	Founded	Revenue (US$)	Number of Employees	Global Operation
ADM	1902	$89 billion	39,000	75 countries
Bunge	1818	$67 billion	35,000	40 countries
Cargill	1865	$136 billion	142,000	66 countries
Louis Dreyfus	1851	$63 billion	22,000	90 countries

Sources: Murphy, Sophia, Burch, David, and Clapp, Jennifer (2012), *Cereal Secrets: The World's Largest Grain Traders and Global Agriculture*, Oxford: Oxfam Research Reports; Clapp, Jennifer (2015), "ABCD and Beyond: From Grain Merchants to Agricultural Value Chain Managers," *Canadian Food Studies* 2(2): 126–35.

1900s with roots in North America and Europe – ADM and Cargill in the US, Bunge in the Netherlands, and Louis Dreyfus in France. Table 1.2 shows the size and geographic reach of these companies. The economic activities of these companies are widespread as well, as Jennifer Clapp has noted: "They buy and sell grain as well as a host of other agricultural and non-agricultural commodities, while they also undertake a range of activities from finance to production to processing and distribution."7 The ABCDs control about 70 percent of the global grain market, though they face growing competition from new companies in Asia, including Noble Group, Olam, and Wilmar, which are three Singapore-listed agribusinesses; Cofco in China; and Glencore Xtrata in Switzerland. Global agrifood companies like these and the ABCDs have used their economic power to shape the rules of the global food system, thereby influencing trends in the production, consumption, and trade of grains across the globe.

Why are these grains so dominant and ubiquitous? What political conflicts and economic processes underlie this dominance? Who controls the world's supply of grains? And, how important are the differences between grains? Many attempts to answer such questions focus on production levels, technology, or the role of large-scale agrifood corporations. Whether trying to explain the contours of the global food system, the eruption of economic conflicts in grain markets, world hunger, the use of biotechnology in grain production, or access to land, the focus is often on production levels, technology, or agrifood corporations. These foci are important to answering these questions, but such explanations also miss the fundamental role that differences between grains can play in such issues.

This book traces the political and economic influence of grains and their role in geopolitical conflicts. In doing so, it examines how competition and conflicts *between different kinds of grains* shape the global food system, the emergence of conflicts in grain markets, trends in world hunger, the use of biotechnology in grain production, and access to land. The market positions and political contexts of different grains intimately shape the economic interests and policy preferences of producers – as well as agrifood corporations. Such differences frequently lead producers of one grain to advocate political policies opposed by producers of other grains. For example, the world wheat market is much more competitive than the market for maize, which is dominated by the US. These divergent market structures have led to different policy preferences for US wheat and maize producers regarding export subsidies, national regulation, and liberalization. Emphasizing such potential divisions brings a new focus to the geopolitics of grains.

Differences in Grains

Despite sharing important similarities, maize, rice, and wheat diverge in a number of important ways, including how they are consumed, where they are grown, and how they are traded. These differences can lead to political and economic conflicts that are, at root, fights over divergent policy preferences that occasionally erupt into violence. Given the importance of such divisions between grains, then, understanding the sources of divisions is imperative. Though there are many potential sources of divisions, three stand out as being particularly consequential: differences in how grains are used, where grains are produced and traded, and the policy preferences connected to grains. Each of these sources of divisions among grains has an important influence on the broader political and economic context.

How We Use Grains

Maize, rice, and wheat differ in a number of ways, but the most important difference is, perhaps, in how they are used. People use these grains in overlapping ways, as food, livestock feed, and even as energy sources. Nevertheless, some grains are almost exclusively consumed directly by people, while other grains are used primarily for feed for livestock. Rice and wheat are food grains that serve as the dietary foundation for most societies and feed most of the world's population. The world production of rice and wheat in 2015 was a significant increase over 1990 (see Table 1.1). Together, rice and wheat are the staple food for most of the people in the world. Even this commonality, though, can be a source of division between grains as rice and wheat producers sometimes find themselves in competition for markets.

World maize production has surpassed all other grains every year since 1998, and it is used in a greater variety of ways than are rice and wheat. Some maize is used in foods in obvious ways, such as cornmeal. Much of the maize produced in the world, however, is used as a central ingredient in a large variety of processed foods. As already noted, maize can be found in such processed foods as bread, coffee creamer, crackers, ketchup, syrup, salad dressing, ice cream, and many,

many more. But maize is also consumed as a central dietary grain, much like rice and wheat, in diets in Latin America and elsewhere. While some maize is consumed directly, much of the maize produced in the world is used for livestock feed. The other grains regularly used for feed include barley, oats, and sorghum. Maize is the primary feed grain in the US, where it accounts for more than 90 percent of total feed grain production and use.

In addition to maize, soybeans are also a primary ingredient in livestock feed. Although soybeans are a legume or oilseed rather than a grain, per se, I discuss soybeans with maize as feed grains in this book for several reasons. First, in many regions where farmers grow maize, soybeans are a rotation crop. Therefore, maize and soybeans share much in the way of production, particularly in where they are produced. Second, a large percentage of world maize and soybean production is used in livestock feed; that is, these two crops are the primary components of animal feed. Third, the division between grains used for food and grains used for feed is perhaps the most important split among grains. Thus, it is no small point that maize and soybeans are the two main components in feed. According to the Food and Agricultural Organization (FAO) of the United Nations, 60 billion chickens, 1.4 billion pigs, and almost 300 million cows were slaughtered for meat in 2013. Such an expansive livestock industry requires immense amounts of feed. In this sense, we consume grains indirectly through eating animals that have been fed a diet based primarily on maize and soybeans. Consequently, I refer to both maize and soybeans as "feed grains."

Since soybeans will be an important part of the discussion of feed grains in this book, a little more information about soy is useful. First, world soybean production puts it near maize, rice, and wheat. In 2015, world soybean production reached 319 MMT. While that is substantially lower than world maize

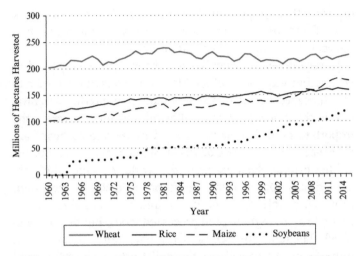

Figure 1.1. World Production for Maize, Rice, Soybeans, and Wheat, 1960–2015.

Source: Foreign Agricultural Service, USDA, "PS&D Online Database."

or wheat production, it is closer to world rice production than it is to other grains, such as barley. Additionally, world soybean production has expanded dramatically over the past 25 years, increasing from 104 MMT in 1990 to 174 MMT in 2000, and then to 319 MMT in 2015. That is an increase of 70 percent from 1990 to 2000, and then 83 percent from 2000 to 2015. From 1990 to 2015, as Figure 1.1 shows, the number of soybean hectares harvested increased from 50 million to 120 million. Second, as with maize, soybeans are used in a wide variety of processed foods. Soy also appears in diets as a central source of protein as a bean, tofu, and soymilk, among many other products. Nevertheless, and again like maize, most of the world soybean production goes into animal feed. Each year, approximately 85 percent of world soybean production is processed ("crushed") into soybean meal and oil. More than 90 percent of soybean meal is used in livestock feed. Therefore, as with maize, there is a clear connection between soybeans and the meat industry.[8]

In recent years, maize has also been increasingly used in yet another way: as a biofuel. Many observers have pointed to the increased use of maize as a biofuel as playing a central role in the global food crisis of 2008. For now, however, the important point is how the uses of maize and soybeans are more varied than for rice or wheat. While maize and soybeans are the primary feed grains in the world, rice and wheat are the primary food grains. This is not to discount the extent to which people consume maize and soybeans directly, for example as an ingredient in processed foods. But the extent to which the grains are used as food versus feed is of paramount importance. As we will see, these distinctions are telling and have important consequences.

The Geography of Grains
In addition to differences in how we use them, these grains also differ regarding where they are produced. It is important to see where different grains are produced, and how that geography of production fits with the distribution of power in the interstate system. The core of the world economy includes nations that hold economic and political dominance. Producers in those nations have a greater ability to protect their interests in the world economy. By contrast, nations outside of the core – in the semi-periphery and especially in the periphery of the world economy – wield substantially less international political and economic influence. Where nations fall in this international hierarchy indicates their international influence. Consequently, the geography of grain production and trade matters tremendously.[9]

In considering the global production of grains, we can see distinct patterns emerge in terms of grain production and, especially, grain exports. In 2015, most of the world's wheat was produced in China, the European Union (EU), India, Russia, and the US, which combined to account for 67 percent of world wheat production that year. The world's top rice producers in 2015 were Bangladesh, China, India, Indonesia, and Vietnam, which together accounted for 73 percent of the world's rice production that year. Brazil, China, the EU, and the US accounted for 73 percent of world maize production in 2015. Not evident in the top four maize producers, though, is a clear link to the Americas: the US is the leading producer of maize, and the US, Argentina, Brazil, and Mexico produced 49 percent of the world's maize in 2015. The world's top soybean producers were Argentina, Brazil, and the US, which together accounted for 83 percent of production in 2015. While China is an important producer of three grains (maize, rice, and wheat), geographic patterns in grain production still emerge. Rice production is anchored in Asia, maize and soybean production is anchored in the US and Latin America, and wheat production is anchored in Europe and North America. This is a central part of the geopolitics of grains.

Another aspect of the geopolitics of grains is the international grain trade, or how grains circulate around the globe. In contrast to world grain production, China is not a major exporter of any of these three major grains. In fact, China was the biggest importer of rice and soybeans in 2015, and it also had substantial maize and wheat imports. In 2015, the US, Brazil, Ukraine, and Argentina were the biggest exporters of maize, together accounting for 86 percent of world exports. Argentina, Brazil, and the US accounted for 88 percent of world exports of soybeans. The major rice exporters were India, Thailand, Vietnam, Pakistan, and the US, which together accounted for 81 percent of world exports. And finally, the major wheat exporters were the US, the EU, Canada, Australia, Russia, and Ukraine, which accounted for

81 percent of world exports that year. With grain exports, then, we can see distinct geographic regions even more clearly. As with world production, maize and soybean exports tend to originate from North and South America, rice exports tend to emerge from Asia, and wheat exports emerge from North America and Europe. The US is the common exporter for each of the grains, and it is the dominant exporter of maize.

We can also look at the percent exported of total production of each grain. Different portions of world production for these grains were exported in 2015: 41 percent of soybeans, 22 percent of wheat, 12 percent of maize, and 9 percent of rice. Farmers who grow crops for export may develop different, and competing, economic interests relative to farmers who do not rely on export markets. Additionally, the world wheat market is more competitive than are the markets for maize or rice. In 2015, while the top four wheat-exporting countries accounted for only 57 percent of world exports, the other grain markets were less competitive: for maize, four exporting countries accounted for 85 percent of world exports; for rice, four exporting countries accounted for 73 percent of world exports; and for soybeans, three countries accounted for 88 percent of world exports. Such differences in the level of competition in markets can also lead to different economic interests and policy preferences. For example, in very competitive markets, producers may seek protection from international competition, such as subsidies or tariffs. Such policy preferences may put those producers at odds with others who face little international competition.

Let's return for a moment to the central division of food grains and feed grains, and see how feed grains, in particular, fit into the geography of production and trade. The US and Brazil are the primary producers and exporters of soybeans and maize, and these two countries dominate the export markets for these commodities. In 2015, the US and Brazil together accounted for 59 percent of world maize exports and 78 percent of world soybean exports. The one difference between maize and soybeans is the percent of world production exported – 12 percent for maize, and 41 percent for soybeans. While China is also a leading producer of both maize and soybeans, it exports neither. In fact, China was by far the world's biggest importer of soybeans in 2015, importing 85 MMT. The EU was a distant second, importing 13 MMT of soybeans. This geography of production and trade for soybeans reaffirms the connection to maize as a central component of feed grain. Discussing maize and soybeans as feed grains makes sense not only because of their common usage, but also because they are similar in their geography of production and trade.

Whereas feed grains are produced and exported primarily by the US and Brazil, food grains have more competitive world markets with more countries exporting rice and wheat. These differences – how the grains are used, where they are produced, and who exports them – are important. Even today, in an age when the political and economic power of agrifood corporations has increased, such differences still matter: the ABCDs, based in North America and Europe, face increased competition from corporations based in Asia. In fact, these differences provide the basis for fundamental disagreements between producers and traders of different grains. These differences have driven some of the most important political and economic currents in world history over the past several centuries.

Divisions Between Grains and National Policies
Conflicting interests between grains often derive from or lead to struggles over national policies, particularly agricultural policy. At a basic level, agricultural policy might be thought of as being on a continuum of policies oriented toward national

regulation at one end and policies oriented toward the market at the other end. For much of the twentieth century, most countries had agricultural policies that reflected the US policy of supply management. This policy included a number of regulations and supports by national governments, usually centering on three programs: price supports, production controls, and export subsidies. After explaining these programs a bit further, we will take a brief look at how divisions between grains contributed to and were caused by supply management policy.

Price supports offer farmers a guaranteed minimum price for particular commodities, effectively regulating market prices in agriculture. Price supports are generally calculated based on volume. For example, rice farmers might receive a guaranteed price for each metric ton. Therefore, a farmer producing 750 MT of rice would receive a greater subsidy from price supports than a farmer who produced 300 MT. Nevertheless, the point of price supports is to increase farm income and stabilize markets in a relatively direct way. More recently, some nations have begun to support farm income more directly with farm subsidies that do not work through or affect the level of prices. When a particular commodity is covered by price supports, it can influence whether farmers grow the grain at all and how much they grow. That is, price supports can shape farmers' economic interests.

Production controls regulate the amount of particular commodities that farmers could produce. Sometimes, production controls take the form of acreage allotments, limiting the amount of land that can be used in producing a particular crop. Other times, marketing agreements limit farmers on how much of a commodity they can bring to market. Whether in the form of acreage allotments, marketing agreements, or other forms, production controls aim to regulate and stabilize production by reducing instances of overproduction and surplus. Production controls sometimes create a stable reserve of commodities by taking surplus gains off the market through marketing agreements, for example, and putting that surplus in storage for use during periods of shortage. Production controls were ended in the US in the 1990s, and many other countries have likewise ended such programs. While they were in place, however, production controls were the corner-stone of supply management policy.

Export subsidies provide support to companies exporting grains. This support gives a competitive advantage to farmers and grain companies from a particular country. For example, the US used export subsidies for wheat beginning in 1954. These subsidies lowered the price of wheat that was exported to Latin America and Asia. This allowed the US to more effec-tively compete with other wheat-exporting countries, such as Canada and Australia, for markets in Japan and elsewhere. Export subsidies also reduced the price of US wheat relative to wheat or other grains produced in the export market (e.g., rice in Japan). By operating in this manner, export subsidies cre-ated a number of potential conflicts between producers and traders of grains in different nations (e.g., US wheat produc-ers versus EU wheat producers), as well as between producers of different kinds of grains.

The geography and uses of grains led to divergent views of supply management policy. In particular, food grain producers – that is, rice and wheat producers – tended to favor supply management policy during the twentieth century. By contrast, feed grain producers were less supportive of supply manage-ment policy. However, where maize was grown as food, such as in Mexico, producers tended to favor supply management, just as other food grain producers did. A few different factors contributed to the split between food grains and feed grains in how supply management was viewed. First, food grain pro-ducers tend to have an interest in higher grain prices, such

as through price supports, because that is the primary deter-
minant of farm income. For feed grain producers, however,
their crops are an input rather than directly consumed by
people. And when feed grain farmers also raise animals for
meat, this means that the farmers have even less interest in
higher prices for maize or soybeans as feed. Second, the varying levels of competition in export markets also matter. With
several nations exporting, competition tended to be higher
in world food grain markets than in world feed grain markets. This meant a greater chance of volatility in prices and
access to markets. Consequently, food grain producers were
more likely to support the regulation and coordination found
in supply management policy. But, feed grain producers and
exporting nations had less interest in such coordination.[10]

The differences in the economic interests of grains – based
especially on how grains are used and where the grains are
produced and consumed – strongly influence the national
policies that producers support and oppose. And since grains
often differ along these lines, producers of different grains
can find themselves pitted against and battling, to varying
degrees, producers of other grains. Sometimes these divisions
occur within nations, and sometimes these divisions occur
across nations.

How Differences in Grains Matter

How are these differences in usage, geography of production, and political preferences important in understanding
our global food system? This book answers that question by
illustrating how divisions among grains influence shifts in
the global food system, economic competition and conflicts
between grains, world hunger, the use of biotechnology in
grain production, and access to land. Chapters 2 and 3 examine the influence of grains on the global food system, or the

international food regime composed of the rules, regulations, and policies that guide agricultural production, trade, and consumption in the world economy. Chapter 2 examines the food regime set by the US between 1945 and 1975. This food regime rested on supply management policy and helped to stabilize agriculture and food in the world economy. Countries across the globe adopted supply management policy, and a variety of international institutions, organizations, and agreements regulated the world economy and encouraged or even required cooperation among nations. One important example was the International Wheat Agreement (IWA), which coordinated global wheat production, prices, and trade. Chapter 2 shows how food grains, particularly wheat, dominated the US food regime. It also shows how divisions between grains shaped the food regime and contributed to its demise. Furthermore, this food regime created a context that facilitated the rise of transnational agrifood corporations, which also contributed to the demise of the US food regime and the spread of liberalization.

Chapter 3 examines the period of liberalization in the world economy that followed the decline of the US food regime after 1975. The regulatory mechanisms of the US food regime, including national policies of supply management and international commodity agreements, were dismantled during this period. In their place came new governing arrangements such as the World Trade Organization (WTO) and its Agreement on Agriculture, which aimed at reducing trade barriers in agriculture, and the Cartagena Protocol on Biosafety, which set the rules for trade in genetically engineered (GE) commodities. This period brought increased competition, conflicts, and economic instability that accompanied the search for new markets. While agrifood corporations – including the ABCDs, seed companies like Monsanto, meat processors, food processors, and retailers – have influenced the global food system

since the decline of the US food regime, we also need to consider how divisions between grains relate to this period of
liberalization. To this end, Chapter 3 examines several examples of such conflicts in the pursuit of markets: the trade war
over wheat export subsidies, the fight to include agriculture in
the General Agreement on Tariffs and Trade (GATT), and the
expansion in global meat production and consumption.

Chapter 4 explores how the geopolitics of grains relates
to, and even contributes to, world hunger and food insecurity. Several recent reports and books have tried to address
"the 9 billion people question": How can the world feed the
projected 9 billion people predicted to inhabit the earth in
2050?[11] Implicit in this question is the idea that agricultural
production is the underlying cause of world hunger, if not
today then certainly in the future. Chapter 4 takes issue with
this focus on production, and instead suggests that the geopolitics of grains plays a more important role in hunger and
food security. Several examples help to highlight the role of
grains: the famines in colonial areas in the 1800s and early
1900s, the global food crisis of 2007–8, food security in South
Asia, the expansion of quinoa production and consumption,
and the increase in global meat production and consumption.

Chapter 5 demonstrates how the division between food
grains and feed grains influences the adoption of or resistance to GE crops. Agrifood corporations again play an
important role, with companies such as Monsanto, DuPont,
and Syngenta using biotechnology to increase their profits
and market power. Their role and influence notwithstand-
ing, the effect of divisions among grains has gone somewhat
underexamined. While there has been some public resistance
to GE feed grains, even more public resistance – and hence
corporate reluctance – has been seen around GE food grains.
Although companies have conducted research and developed
GE wheat and rice, no such varieties have yet been marketed

for commercial use. Nor have national governments approved GE food grains for commercial distribution. This chapter argues that considering food grains and feed grains in the context of the world economy is particularly important to understanding the various responses to GE grains.

The book concludes with Chapter 6, which examines the relationship between the geopolitics of grains and access to land. The recent attention to "land grabs" by corporations (e.g., Hassad Food, Terra Firma Capital, and Louis Dreyfus) and various countries (e.g., China, South Korea, and Saudi Arabia) has highlighted the importance of landownership and land rights. Land grabs have been an important source of resistance to the current global food system, as organizations such as La Via Campesina have mobilized peasants and farmers across the globe. Yet the public discussions about land grabs tend to touch on the role of grains only at the surface – corporations and countries often seek to acquire land to grow grains. This chapter looks beyond the surface to examine how divisions among grains play a role in the ebb and flow of land rights over the past 150 years. Since the late 1800s, periods of land expropriation have alternated with periods of land reform, which have widened access to land. This ebb and flow of land rights is linked to the geopolitics of grains.

The Geopolitics of Grains

Through all of these issues – shifts in the global food system, economic competition and conflicts between grains, world hunger, the use of biotechnology in grain production, and access to land – understanding how grains fit into the broader world economic context is crucial. Each grain has geographic roots: maize and soybeans are produced primarily in North and South America, rice is produced primarily in Asia, and wheat is produced primarily by industrialized countries in

North America and Europe. These geographic roots contribute to differences in political power for producers and
corporations, to the extent that influence in global governance
is tied to nation-states and the interstate system.

In this way, we need to understand how grains fit into
the world economy. The international food regime sets the
market, thereby exerting a strong influence over the production, trade, and consumption of grains across the globe. The
food regime is made up of the rules, regulations, and policies
that govern the global production, distribution, and consumption of food and is set by the dominant nation in the world
economy. Over the past 200 years, the British and then the
US set the food regime, but they did so in very different ways.
The British food regime was based primarily on free trade,
while the US food regime rested heavily on the national regulation of agriculture.

While the food regime shapes the production, trade, and
consumption of grains, grains also influence the shape of the
food regime. Wheat, in particular, was central to the formation
of both the British and US food regimes. Maize and rice have
also been important, and this has been especially true as the
US food regime has declined and faltered over the past several decades. In this way, political economic divisions between
grains shape the contours of a food regime. The political coalitions formed by, and economic competition between, maize,
rice, and wheat producers are central elements of the history
of food regimes.[12]

The political divisions and coalitions among grains shift
over time, as do the economic interests and political power of
grain producers and agrifood corporations. Shifts in the world
economy can lead to changes in economic interests connected
to different grains. Karl Polanyi, an economic historian,
discussed the idea of a "double movement of the market,"
whereby the market moves back and forth between the poles

of free market, laissez faire capitalism and a nationally regulated market economy. This double movement is clear where grains are concerned, and throughout this book we will examine how the double movement shapes food regimes, economic competition, world hunger and food security, biotechnology, and access to land. Each chapter will focus on one of these issues. The final chapter, in particular, explores how this double movement has contributed to resistance in the world economy around the issue of access to land, which is a key element in the geopolitics of grains. As the food regime has shifted, so too has people's accessibility to land for cultivation. Chapter 6 explores the ebb and flow of land reform, which increases access through redistribution, and land expropriation, which decreases access through commodification and privatization.[13]

People around the world rely on grains as a core component of their diets, making grains a vital food that frequently shapes individuals' identities and health. Grains also touch many aspects of society: inequality, political power, land rights, and cultural traditions, among many others. Together, this influence on individuals and societies makes grains a potential source of political instability and even violence. But there is also an important global aspect to grains that is revealed by examining closely the economic and political contexts of grain production, consumption, and trade. The following chapters aim to shed light on this complex geopolitics of grains.

CHAPTER TWO

Grains and the US Food Regime

From 1945 through 1975, diets around the world changed in fundamental ways, particularly in terms of grain consumption. At the beginning of the period, the diets in countries in Asia were centered on rice, and Latin American countries had diets that rested on maize. While some wheat was consumed in each of these regions, the other grains dominated diets. Yet by 1975, diets in many countries in Asia and Latin America had changed as the consumption of wheat increased dramatically. Although rice and maize were still central to Asian and Latin American diets respectively, they no longer dwarfed wheat in consumption levels.

We can see this dynamic by looking at one country in each region: Japan in Asia and Colombia in Latin America. In each of these countries, the per capita consumption of the traditional grain – rice and maize, respectively – declined substantially in the 1960s. At the same time, the per capita consumption of wheat increased – and so did US wheat imports into each country. In Japan, per capita rice consumption fell by 21 percent, from about 240 grams per day in 1961 to 189 grams per day in 1971. By contrast, per capita wheat consumption increased from 91 grams per day to 110 grams per day, which is an increase of 17 percent. Similarly, in Colombia, per capita maize consumption fell by 24 percent between 1964 and 1974, from 115 grams per day to 87 grams per day. Meanwhile, wheat consumption rose slightly from 43 grams per day to 48 grams per day between 1963 and 1973, which is an increase of almost 12 percent. More importantly for Colombia, though, was that domestic wheat production dropped precipitously by 62 percent during this period, and the country became more dependent on US wheat imports, which increased by 130 percent. We will discuss the details of the shifts in grains in Japan and Colombia later in the chapter, but for now it is important to see that significant shifts occurred.

How can we explain such shifts in grain consumption? It was driven in part by a shift in US agricultural policy and a concomitant change in the international food regime. In 1954, the US Congress passed the Agricultural Trade Development and Assistance Act, often referred to as Public Law 480 (or, PL 480). This legislation created international food aid, through which the US sent subsidized food and agricultural products to other nations. The import of cheap, subsidized wheat into countries like Japan and Colombia helped to expand wheat consumption, thus contributing to a shift in diets. At the same time, however, this food aid often competed against domestically produced grains – this meant rice in Japan and maize in Colombia.

Ultimately, such shifts in national diets and consumption patterns are driven by the international food regime. A food regime is an overarching global system that governs the production, trade, and consumption of food and agriculture around the world. This includes the rules, regulations, policies, and norms that are created by national governments, as well as international agreements, institutions, and organizations. Food regimes set the market for food in the world economy and guide the shape of agricultural production and trade across the globe, and grains have been central to food regimes for the past 150 years. Two characteristics of food regimes are particularly important: the extent of national regulation and the patterns of trade in basic foodstuffs, especially grains. At times, governments have had national policies that regulated agriculture extensively, from production to prices to trade. At other times, agriculture has been regulated far less, leaving market mechanisms to influence production, prices, and trade. Similarly, grains have flowed toward powerful centers in the world economy (e.g., Europe) at some points in history, and at other points grains have flowed away from these nations to less powerful areas. Regardless of the extent of national regulation or the directions in which food flows, food regimes share an important and fundamental characteristic: a world market that influences prices, production, and the movement of grains across the globe.

Scholars have identified two food regimes. The first food regime was constructed during British world-economic dominance, from about 1860 to about 1914. The second food regime existed during US dominance, from about 1945 to 1975.[1] In each instance, the country that dominated the world economy set the food regime. These two food regimes differed in terms of national regulations and international trade flows. First, in terms of the extent of national regulation, the British food regime was much more market-oriented, relying on free trade. Britain had eliminated its government support for agriculture with the repeal of the Corn Laws in the early 1840s. They constructed an international system of free trade for agriculture – and the world economy, in general – through bilateral free trade agreements. Second, the British food regime involved trade flows that saw grains flow from the periphery of the world economy to the core. That is, grain flowed from Latin America, Asia, Africa, Australia, and North America to Europe, particularly Britain. Some of the geographic origins of grains going to Europe were colonies and some were independent nations. But, the most powerful nations economically, politically, and militarily, tended not to export grains to the periphery.

The US food regime was quite distinct from the British food regime. The US food regime rested heavily on national regulations that influenced agricultural production and set prices. Trade barriers emerged, as well. In addition, the flow of grains was the opposite of what appeared in the British food regime: during the US food regime, grains flowed from the core of the world economy to the periphery. Nations that were powerful economically and politically exported grains to poorer nations. In particular, the US and Europe exported grains to countries in Africa, Asia, and Latin America.

The importance of food regimes can be seen in their consequences. The British food regime changed the structure of agriculture in many parts of the world by imposing plantation systems to facilitate exports back to Britain. This food regime also changed production patterns of agriculture across the globe, and it altered consumption patterns, particularly in Europe and Britain. At its worst, as we will see in Chapter 4, the British food regime contributed to massive famines in places such as India, Brazil, and China. It also led to the expropriation of vast expanses of land from millions of people. Food regimes, then, have the power to shape patterns of agricultural production, trade, and consumption, thereby shaping the lives of farmers and consumers and even the ways in which societies are organized. While the US food regime rested on the national regulation of agricultural production, prices, and trade, it produced many of the same effects seen with the British food regime: changing the patterns of production and consumption around the globe, and even contributing to food insecurity in some instances. Given the strong influence and long reach that food regimes have, understanding how they form and what factors influence their shape is an important endeavor. In particular, understanding the US food regime – how it formed and spread, how it operated, how it collapsed, and the consequences it had – is important for understanding the geopolitics of grains.

This chapter first looks at the US food regime and its origins, which are to be found in national politics during the turmoil of the Great Depression in the 1930s. Then, it examines how the regime spread through international organizations and trade agreements. Next, the chapter explores the consequences of the US food regime for farmers, consumers, national policies, and societies throughout the world. Finally, the chapter closes by looking at how the US food regime collapsed, allowing for the transition to a new food regime, which is still in flux. Maize, rice, and wheat each have central roles in this history of the US food regime, which is clear in its origins.

The US Food Regime and its Origins

The US food regime regulated the production, trade, and consumption of food between about 1945 and 1975. The end years of food regimes are periods of transition, so the beginning and end are difficult to pinpoint. Nonetheless, we can look to markers such as the creation of national policies or the establishment of international agreements and organizations to mark the start and end points. During this period, the US food regime set the market for grains. The regulations and policies constituting this food regime delimited prices and had an incredibly strong influence on patterns of production, trade, and consumption. This is clear for both food grains and feed grains. After looking at the US food regime a little more closely, we will move on to explore its origins.

An Outline of the US Food Regime

In contrast to the British food regime that preceded it, the US food regime rested on the regulation of agricultural production and markets. Nations across the globe adopted, to varying degrees, a policy of supply management that centered on price supports, production controls, and export subsidies. This represented an astounding level of regulation of the market economy. Price supports generally provided minimum, guaranteed prices for farmers; production controls regulated the kinds and quantities of crops produced; and export subsidies facilitated trade below production costs, with the consequence of changing production patterns in export markets and consumption around the world. A few countries – such as the US, Japan, and France – adopted supply management policy in the 1930s, but this policy spread to a large number of countries as US world economic hegemony was established through various trade agreements and international organizations. Countries in Europe, North and South America, and Asia all adopted supply management policy, as did countries that were newly emerging from colonial empires in Africa and Southeast Asia. Supply management policy – with its regulation of prices, production, and trade – became the standard and accepted national agricultural policy around the world by the 1960s. This is clearly a sharp turn from the free trade and laissez faire foundation upon which the British food regime rested.

But the regulation of agriculture did not stop at national policies. At the level of the world economy, international commodities agreements formed to regulate wheat, coffee, cocoa, and a few other commodities. These agreements aimed to coordinate markets by regulating production, trade, and prices. The International Wheat Agreement (IWA), for instance, brought together the leading wheat-producing and wheat-consuming nations with the aim of stabilizing supply and prices. These nations agreed on minimum and maximum prices for set quantities of wheat. The first IWA went into effect in 1949 and was renegotiated seven times over the next 20 years. The IWA did not regulate all wheat traded in the world economy but only a portion of it, and other grains – most notably maize and rice – did not have such international agreements. Maize, rice, and other grains were regulated by national policies of supply management but were not coordinated internationally in the same way as was wheat. Still, the IWA continued to regulate the world wheat market until 1970, when it was changed and weakened. Thus, agriculture was regulated extensively, nationally and sometimes internationally, in terms of production, prices, and trade during the height of the US food regime.

Why did the food regime change so dramatically from what it had been during British hegemony? How can we explain the shape of each of these food regimes, especially that of the US? We first need to recognize that grains play an important role in the formation of food regimes. The contours of both the British and US food regimes were intimately shaped by the politics of grains, including how producers of different grains related to one another, and how grain producers related to other agricultural producers, such as livestock or cotton producers. That is, grains played a central role in the political coalitions and divisions in agriculture that shaped national policies and hence influenced the food regimes.

For example, agricultural politics within Britain shaped the food regime in the 1800s, with its emphasis on the free market. Grain producers in Britain favored protections against foreign competition and helped to institute the Corn Laws. The Importation Act of 1815 was at the heart of the Corn Laws, and it severely restricted the importation of grains into Britain by imposing steep import tariffs. In the early 1800s, other countries – France, Germany, and the US, among others – also had tariffs. As Britain became the dominant world power and sought to liberalize the world economy, it did so first by opening its own borders. This meant eliminating the Corn Laws, which it did through the Importation Act of 1846. This was part of the basis of British free trade as it opened the British market to wheat imports, which increased from

0.2 MMT in 1845 to more than 1.3 MMT in 1860 and averaged 2.3 MMT per year in the 1870s. British wheat imports increased steadily from 1850 to 1910, when they reached 5.3 MMT. In the span of a few decades, then, Britain became the world's largest wheat importer.[2]

This repeal of the Corn Laws set the stage for free trade in agriculture throughout the world economy, but how did it come about? In part, there was a political division between agriculture and industry in Britain. While grain producers favored the Corn Laws, opposition emerged from a variety of industries, including textiles, steel, iron, and manufacturing. But, there is more to the establishment of the free trade food regime than agriculture versus industry. Divisions within agriculture also played a key role in this policy shift. Grain producers favored the Corn Laws because they reduced competition from imports and kept domestic grain prices high. Livestock producers, however, increasingly opposed the Corn Laws. By maintaining agricultural tariffs, the Corn Laws kept prices relatively high for livestock producers' main input: grain. Consequently, livestock farmers – especially cattle producers – gave their support to repealing the Corn Laws. Thus, a political division between food grains and feed grains intimately shaped the British food regime.[3]

Similar dynamics can be seen in the formation of the US food regime, as coalitions and divisions between producers of food grains and feed grains shaped the formation of the food regime as well as its demise.

The Chaotic Origins of the US Food Regime

The US food regime had its origins in the global economic chaos of the early twentieth century. When the British food regime broke down in the early 1900s, agriculture became increasingly unstable in the world economy, as production patterns changed and prices became more volatile. The changes in production and greater instability in prices, of course, are linked. This was most evident in the 1920s, when other sectors of the world economy were doing relatively well. That is to say, agriculture experienced instability and entered the depression before the rest of the world economy. As farmers and governments attempted to ameliorate this economic turmoil, many of them turned toward policies of supply management to help regulate production and prices.

One root of the economic problems for agriculture was the increase in production for various commodities and in many countries around the world during the 1920s. To a great extent, this expansion in grain production was a consequence of the First World War, during which European agriculture declined significantly. For example, after averaging about 9 MMT annually from 1900 to 1912, wheat production in France dropped to about 5.8 MMT per year from 1914 to 1918 and remained only slightly higher for the years immediately after the war. From 1913 to 1917, Russian wheat production also dropped off dramatically, by 34 percent from 27.9 MMT to 16.9 MMT. In all, annual wheat production in Europe (not including Russia) averaged 35 MMT from 1909 to 1913 but fell to an average of 27.7 MMT from 1914 to 1918, a decline of 21.4 percent. Consequently, the war presented an opportunity for other countries to expand their grain production and exports.[4]

During the war, grain production increased in North and South America, Africa, and Asia. Despite wheat production falling in Europe by 9.8 MMT and in Russian by 11 MMT between 1913 and 1918, world wheat production fell by only 5.3 MMT. Several countries saw their wheat production increase during the war: Argentina, Australia, Canada, India, and the US. When European agriculture recovered after the war, however, agricultural production in other countries and regions did not decline. In fact, average annual wheat production in the 1920s for those countries just listed remained

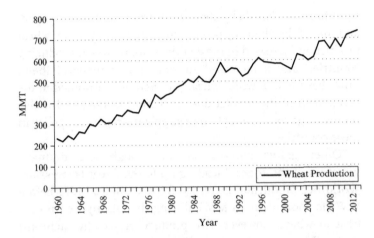

Figure 2.1. World Wheat Production, 1960–2015.

Source: Foreign Agricultural Service, USDA, "PS&D Online Database."

above the averages before the war – sometimes double the annual pre-war average.

As Figure 2.1 shows, world wheat production hovered around 100 MMT by the late 1920s, which was substantially higher than the annual average of about 79 MMT from 1905 to 1913. World wheat production rose fairly steadily from 1920 when it totaled about 86.7 MMT to 1932 when it was 105.5 MMT in the depth of the Great Depression – an increase of almost 22 percent. During this time, wheat production increased in several nations, including Argentina, Australia, Canada, the US, and especially the Soviet Union. For example, Soviet wheat production recovered slowly from the war and revolution, averaging only 10 MMT per year from 1920 to 1924. By contrast, Soviet wheat production increased dramatically in the last part of the decade to average about 22 MMT from 1925 to 1932. Other countries also saw increased wheat production during the 1920s: Argentina by about 80 percent between 1922 and 1928, Australia by about 70 percent from

1922 to 1932, Canada by about 85 percent from 1921 to 1928, and the US by about 14 percent from 1921 to 1931. So, wheat production increased in most of the primary wheat-producing countries, and it increased substantially in many of them. This sharp rise in world wheat production contributed to the breakdown of the market due to overproduction, and it also set the stage for the adoption of supply management policy in these countries.

"Other grains showed similar though less dramatic increases in the 1920s," leading up to the Great Depression. World rice production increased from about 49 MMT before WWI to more than 58 MMT during the late 1920s. In contrast to wheat, however, rice production actually increased during WWI, in part because the war was not centered in rice-producing nations. The war did reach part of China as Japan took over some of Germany's colonial holdings in China, but even this battle was relatively brief. At this time, much of Asia was colonized: India and Burma by the British, Indochina by the French, the Philippines by the US, and Korea and Taiwan by Japan. Several countries colonized parts of China: France, Germany, Great Britain, Japan, Russia/USSR, and the US.

Colonization had important implications for rice production. For example, as Japan and western nations colonized Asia in the late 1800s and early 1900s, they provided the "infrastructure for the opening up of new land, constructing canals which served the dual purpose of draining marshy areas so that they became cultivable and providing easy access by water so that the produce could be shipped out."[5] This, of course, meant increased rice production and exports. In fact, the major rice-exporting areas were under colonial control: Burma, India, Indochina, and Thailand. This expansion continued past the depression. For example, following WWI, Japan encouraged the expansion of rice production in its colonies as well as domestically. Thus, markets within Asia for rice exports remained despite the depression: "The exports of rice from mainland southeast Asia rose from an annual average of 5.4 million metric tons in the late 1920s to 5.9 million metric tons in the early 1930s, and fell back only slightly to 5.7 million in the late 1930s."[6] Nonetheless, the effects of the depression were deep and lingered after the Second World War for some rice-producing countries: "When the Depression hit Asia and the demand for rice suddenly contracted, in Southeast Asia the resulting surpluses of rice made for a devastating fall in prices, severe impoverishment, communal strife, and a stagnation of the rural economy which in Burma and Thailand lasted well into the 1950s."[7] "This is in large part because exports to some markets decreased substantially." Japanese rice imports, in particular, fell from an average of 0.4 MMT between 1925 and 1929 to an average of 0.1 MMT between 1930 and 1934.[8]

In Asia, the push for supply management policy during the 1920s and 1930s was most visible in Japan, which received increasing rice imports from the areas it had colonized in Asia. Before the war, rice production was about 0.65 MMT in Taiwan and 1.5 MMT in Korea. But rice production had risen significantly by the late 1920s in these Japanese colonies: to more than 0.9 MMT in Taiwan, and about 2.2 MMT in Korea. This is in addition to the increase in Japanese rice production, from about 7.2 MMT before the war to about 8.5 MMT in the late 1920s. Consequently, Japan and other Asian countries used import controls. They also instituted government purchase programs that aimed to raise prices, similar to US price supports. Unlike price supports in the US, however, the Japanese policy also intended to increase domestic rice production. In the Philippines and Siam (Thailand), the governments created corporations to purchase and distribute rice, thereby bypassing rice merchants and traders. However, rice-producing countries confronted some of the same issues as wheat-producing countries by the early 1930s.[9]

World maize production increased from about 135 MMT before WWI to more than 150 MMT during the late 1920s. The US was the leading producer of maize, accounting for 53–65 percent of world production between 1918 and 1929. Argentina was the biggest exporter of maize, however, while the US was a distant second. As with wheat, maize production in Europe dropped off during WWI, falling from about 20 MMT in 1914 to 11 MMT in 1918. Similarly, maize production plummeted in Russia during this same time. During WWI, Argentina exported grains to France and Italy. Argentina expanded its grain production beginning in 1918, and maize production increased from 7 MMT in 1920 to 13 MMT in 1930. Maize production in Brazil was very small prior to WWI, but increased sharply immediately following the war and remained at about 6 MMT through the 1920s. Perhaps most importantly, European maize production recovered and expanded significantly during the 1920s, increasing from about 18 MMT in 1920 to more than 28 MMT in 1932.[10]

This increased production contributed to surpluses of wheat, maize, rice, and many other agricultural commodities. This ultimately contributed to instability in prices and clogged export markets in the world economy. The effects of the trends in production can be seen in agricultural prices, which were unstable in the 1920s and had an overall downward trajectory. In the US, grain prices fell sharply between 1926 and 1932: the price of maize fell from $0.71 per bushel to $0.32, and wheat fell from $1.21 per bushel to $0.38. In 1926, rice prices also began to fall as rice production expanded: "Rangoon No. 2 (rice) fell from over £0.70 per cwt in 1927, to below £0.30 per cwt in 1933."[11] Farm incomes plummeted along with the sharp decline in agricultural price. Grain farmers around the world reacted to declining prices with a similar response: increase production. Of course, this response only exacerbated the turmoil in world agricultural markets by increasing the supply of grains and further depressing prices.

In the midst of clogged world markets, declining and unstable prices, and overproduction and surpluses, countries attempted to find solutions. Many countries turned to high tariffs to restrict imports from further reducing domestic agricultural prices and hurting farmers' incomes. A few countries – including Argentina, France, Japan, and the US – turned to policies of supply management, which aimed to reduce production and raise prices by paying farmers to limit their production. This may seem like an odd policy since people around the world, including in the US, were suffering from hunger. Beyond wreaking havoc in agriculture in terms of prices, the Great Depression brought sharp declines in incomes in industry and on the farm, as well as sharply increased unemployment and poverty. Still, the establishment of supply management policy in the US was of particular importance, as this country set the food regime in the middle of the twentieth century.

This turn to national regulation, however, was neither automatic nor inevitable. Rather, supply management policy emerged out of political battles. In the US during the 1920s, for example, organizations and politicians representing wheat and maize farmers tried several times to establish a policy of supply management that would support farm income and help to regulate production. But, they failed repeatedly. The McNary–Haugen bills of 1924, 1926, 1927, and 1928 each proposed to raise agricultural prices by having the government purchase surplus commodities, sell them abroad at world prices, and protect domestic prices with a tariff. The basic aim of the bills was to manage the supply of commodities and prevent overproduction. However, each attempt to enact the bill failed: in 1924 and 1926, the bill failed to win enough votes to pass both the House and Senate; and in

1927 and 1928, the bill passed the House and the Senate only to be vetoed by President Coolidge each time. Therefore, there was not enough political power to pass the legislation and create supply management policy. This was largely because the political coalition favoring supply management in the US did not initially include an important segment of agriculture: cotton farmers (especially plantation owners) in the South. And even when the political coalition included cotton, maize, and wheat growers – as it did in 1927 and 1928 – it did not wield enough influence in the presidential administration to create this policy.

The election of Franklin Roosevelt in 1932 and the enactment of the New Deal brought supply management as US agricultural policy. The Agricultural Adjustment Act (AAA) of 1933 established price supports and production controls as the core programs of US agricultural policy. Price supports aimed to boost farm income, and production controls aimed to prevent large surpluses. Thus, supply management became the basis of US agricultural policy, and behind this policy shift was a coalition of maize, wheat, and cotton farmers.

The economic interests of these farmers coincided around price supports and production controls, and their collective political power was crucial to the passage of the AAA, which created supply management policy. Most importantly, southern planters and Democrats came to advocate strongly for supply management policy. Roosevelt's administration included many supporters of supply management from the Wheat Belt and Corn Belt, and it relied heavily on southern Democrats who controlled both the House and the Senate. Once the cotton–maize–wheat coalition dominated the House and Senate and held sway in the presidential administration, then supply management policy was created.

This story of overproduction in the 1920s and the creation of supply management policy in the 1930s played out in a handful of countries around the world, including Canada, France, and Japan. In the 1920s and 1930s, Japan faced an overproduction of rice, in part from its colonies, Korea and Formosa. In 1933, Japan passed the Rice Control Law, which regulated imports and created a system of buying domestic rice, established a sliding scale of minimum prices across the year, and created a reserve to stabilize the price and availability of rice. That is, Japan sought to manage the supply of rice.

Australia attempted to counteract slumping agricultural prices during the Great Depression with price subsidies, but this country did not create supply management policy including production controls until after WWII. In Argentina, grain farmers threatened to leave the 1933–4 crops unharvested. This led the government to introduce a Grain Regulation Board that offered minimum prices for maize, wheat, and flaxseed. Grain farmers across the globe pushed for protections from the market, particularly in the form of price supports. Likewise, governments in several nations developed policies with the aim of stabilizing – and maintaining – grain production levels. As the market economy became more volatile and began to break down, grain farmers sought protections from the market.

In countries that adopted supply management between 1920 and 1950, this policy was generally the result of a coalition of farmers – particularly food grain farmers – and left-wing labor parties and organizations. In the US, for example, this meant the New Deal coalition of maize and wheat farmers, southern cotton farmers, and northern labor unions. In Japan immediately following WWII, a coalition of farmers and left-wing organizations threatened a social revolution aimed at creating a social democracy. The rural radicalism spurred by the Great Depression was the central force in forging supply management policy. Similar dynamics were at work in other countries, including Australia, Canada, France, and several others.

While a number of countries enacted policies of supply management in the 1920s and 1930s, the spread and solidification of this policy really occurred through the establishment of the US food regime. After 1945, most countries around the world adopted some version of price supports and production controls. How did this happen? Why did countries adopt supply management policy during this particular period? The answers to these questions rest in the construction of the US food regime.

The Spread of the US Food Regime

The US food regime was established through international organizations and agreements. First, in 1947, the US led the way in creating the General Agreement on Tariffs and Trade (GATT), which was the vehicle for multilateral negotiations on economic matters. GATT had an important role in the spread of the US food regime. Second, international commodity agreements were formed to regulate world markets for some commodities. Each of these elements contributed to the creation of a context in which nations were effectively encouraged to adopt supply management policy, especially where grains were concerned.

First, GATT facilitated the worldwide spread of supply management. One primary aim of the US after WWII was to liberalize the world economy. During the depression and the war, economic barriers rose around the globe. The US aimed to reduce these barriers through GATT, which consisted of periodic multilateral trade talks and established the principle of Most Favored Nation (MFN) trading status. The number of nations participating in GATT talks increased with each round. MFN required that any trade preferences given to one nation must be given to all nations. One primary target of this trade system was the British system of imperial preferences.

In this system, countries and colonies that were members of the British Commonwealth had protections from international competition and imports, but they also had preferential trade status with other Commonwealth members. The US wanted access to these markets and, therefore, sought to end this system of imperial preferences.

While the US pushed for a more liberal and open world economy through GATT, there was one economic sector that GATT left exempt from this push: agriculture. Article XI of GATT prohibited tariff restrictions, except when "used in support of certain domestic agricultural programs, particularly those which, by raising domestic prices above the world market price, tend to create an incentive for importation." This exemption applied only when such barriers were needed to enforce state policies that imposed limits on domestic sales or production, or "to remove a temporary surplus of the like domestic product."[12] In addition, Article XVI of GATT permitted export subsidies for agricultural products. All of this meant that GATT allowed for supply management policy, even at the expense of creating a more liberal and open world economy.

As the US established supply management as the core of its agricultural policy, the level of support and economic intervention in terms of price supports and production controls increased substantially. As we have seen, the level of government support for agriculture in the US expanded dramatically from the 1930s through the 1950s. Furthermore, the production of grains in the US increased as the use of technology increased, farms became larger and more concentrated, and supply management encouraged greater productivity and production. In other words, the US produced more food grains and feed grains, and increased the amount of support given to this production. Therefore, other nations had to adopt similar policies to compete with the growth of subsidized grains produced in US agriculture. This meant that more and more nations adopted policies that favored farmers, encouraged greater production, and restricted imports.

Following the Second World War, plans were put forth to create an International Trade Organization (ITO), which would set forth and enforce international rules of trade. The ITO did not come to fruition because agricultural interests – particularly wheat and cotton farmers – in the US feared that such an international organization would push for greater liberalization in agriculture and call for the end of supply management policy. Therefore, wheat farmers shaped international politics to allow for their favored policy, which did not match the policy preferences of all agricultural producers. This is particularly evident when we compare how the food regime changed at the end of the twentieth century: with the establishment of the World Trade Organization (WTO) to help push for liberalization in agriculture, in part reflecting the interests of feed grains. For the time being, however, the important point is that the failure to create the ITO in the 1940s further facilitated the spread of supply management policy across the globe.

The second aspect of the US food regime facilitating the spread of supply management policy was international commodity agreements, which regulated international prices, production, and trade in certain agricultural commodities. In other words, international commodity agreements instilled the principles and policies of supply management at the level of the world economy. A handful of agricultural commodities were subject to international commodity agreements, the most important of which were cocoa, coffee, and especially wheat. In 1949, the International Wheat Agreement (IWA) came into effect and established minimum and maximum prices "at which 'guaranteed quantities' of wheat [would] be offered by designated exporting countries or purchased by designated importing countries."[13] The IWA brought together the major wheat-exporting and wheat-importing countries to coordinate the supply and price of wheat, with the aim of stabilizing the international wheat market. The leading wheat-exporting countries that participated in the IWA included Australia, Canada, and the US, which together accounted for more than 75 percent of exports at the time.

Not all agricultural commodities were subject to international agreements. Neither maize nor rice had such agreements. For rice, there were two major international organizations: the International Rice Commission (IRC), and the International Rice Research Institute (IRRI). The IRC was established by the United Nations in 1949 to "to promote national and international action in matters relating to the production, conservation, distribution and consumption of rice." That is, the IRC worked to facilitate international cooperation regarding the production, distribution, and consumption of rice, but not in terms of international trade. Therefore, the IRC did not establish supply management for rice at the level of the world economy. The IRC may have supported the adoption of such national policies of supply management, but it did not coordinate international rice production, prices, or trade.[14]

Nor did the IRRI work toward establishing supply management policy for rice at the level of the world economy. The IRRI was established in 1960 and focused primarily on research and education. The Ford Foundation and Rockefeller Foundation, in partnership with the government of the Philippines, founded the IRRI to improve rice production. The IRRI was central to the spread of the "Green Revolution," which encouraged and supported farmers to adopt new seed varieties and agricultural technologies to improve production. Toward this goal, then, the IRRI focused on research and education but not working to regulate production, prices, or trade.

In contrast to wheat and rice, there was no international organization representing maize growers during the US food regime. Organizations representing maize farmers in the US advocated for market-oriented policies and liberalization in the world economy. This, of course, was not the common stance of maize farmers around the world. In fact, most maize farmers outside the US favored supply management. Some did so because the maize they grew was used as food rather than livestock feed. For example, in Mexico, smaller farmers in particular tended to favor that country's policies that subsidized maize production and protected the market from imports. The maize that they grew was primarily for human consumption. In addition, they faced competition from US maize growers, who were subsidized. This also prompted Mexican maize farmers to support supply management policy. Maize farmers, such as those in Mexico, may have favored a commodity agreement for maize, except that they did little exporting. The US dominated world maize markets and had little incentive for an international commodity agreement since there was little international competition.

Why were these commodities so different in terms of international organizations and the policies pursued and preferred in the world economy? A significant part of the answer is the extent to which each of these commodities was traded in the world economy. A much greater proportion of world wheat production is circulated through trade. From 1947 to 1975, generally about 20 percent of world wheat production was traded. During this same period, by contrast, only about 10 percent of maize circulated through international trade. More starkly, a mere 4 percent of rice went to export. Therefore, the need for international regulation differed between these three commodities.

Beyond the proportion of world wheat that is exported,

the world wheat market itself helped to lead to the formation of the IWA. The wheat market was – and continues
to be – competitive, with several nations competing for
export markets. Three countries – Australia, Canada, and
the US – dominated the world wheat market, accounting
for about 72 percent of all exports between 1960 and 1975.
Several other countries – including Argentina, France,
and the Soviet Union – accounted for the remainder of
world wheat exports. The most intense competition, however, occurred between the US and Canada. Part of this
competition stemmed not just from the number of exporting nations but also from the closing of some traditional
import markets, particularly Europe. The IWA helped to
carve out new market boundaries, especially for the US
and Canada. With Europe largely closed to wheat imports,
Canada turned to exporting to communist countries in Asia
and Eastern Europe, as well as the Soviet Union in some
years. The US, by contrast, turned to developing countries
in Africa, Asia, and Latin America. The coordination and
regulation imposed by the IWA was viewed as beneficial by
exporting nations, in particular.

The world feed grains markets were far less competitive.
Both the maize and soybean markets were dominated by the
US, which accounted for the majority of feed grain exports.
From 1957 to 1975, the US alone averaged about 58 percent
of world maize exports and would account for more than
70 percent in a few years. The US was even more dominant
in soybean exports during this period, averaging about 85 percent of world exports. During this period, no other country
approached anything close to the US level of exports. Just as
important, export markets for US feed grains were abundant
and included parts of Africa, Asia, Europe, and Latin America.
Consequently, there was little need to coordinate or regulate
international production of or trade in feed grains – at least

not from the US perspective, and that nation set the food regime.

International organizations existed for rice, but these organizations did not coordinate trade or the world rice market, as with the IWA or other commodity agreements. The IRC and IRRI had activities other than coordinating international trade, prices, or production. "This was in large part due to" the small proportion of rice that circulated in international trade: only 4 percent of world rice production went to exports between 1960 and 1975. And, just two countries – Thailand and Burma – often accounted for close to half of all rice exports.

The US food regime facilitated the spread of supply management policy in a couple of ways. First, GATT exempted agriculture from its general push to liberalize the world economy. Countries could maintain trade barriers to limit agricultural imports, and they could also regulate prices and production. Second, some commodities had international commodity agreements, which coordinated international markets by regulating trade, production, and world prices. Wheat was the only grain with such an agreement. Neither maize nor rice was regulated by an international commodity agreement. This was partly because maize and rice had less competitive markets and a smaller portion of world maize and rice production was exported. By contrast, a substantial portion of wheat was exported, and several nations exported wheat, leading to a competitive world market. Wheat producers were politically powerful because of their place within the dominant political coalition in the US, which set the food regime. Consequently, the US food regime accommodated the preferences of wheat producers by allowing supply management policy and international coordination of markets.

The Effects of the US Food Regime

The US food regime, with its goal of establishing cooperation and economic regulation in agriculture in the world economy, had a number of important effects. First, the US food regime facilitated the spread of supply management policy across the globe. As this policy spread, it had implications for agricultural production and farm income. Second, this food regime contributed to increased production of grains that led to surpluses, which were then shipped abroad through export subsidies. Third, this food regime reshaped diets throughout the world. All of these consequences of the US food regime, in an ironic twist, ultimately undermined the regime itself. Before getting to that point, it is first necessary to discuss the effects in more detail.

First, the food regime facilitated the spread of supply management policy to almost every country around the world. Supply management policy could be found in Africa, Asia, Europe, Latin America, North America, and even the Middle East. Some of the highest levels of protection are found in rice-producing countries in Asia, including Japan, South Korea, and Taiwan. Japan, for example, made income parity between agriculture and industry a central goal of its agricultural policy in the 1960s, and it pursued this goal through high price support levels for rice farmers. In addition to price supports and production controls, many countries in Asia used state enterprise organizations in the rice trade: Australia, China, India, Indonesia, Japan, South Korea, Vietnam, and others. There tended to be, then, high levels of protection, high levels of support for farmers, and extensive regulation of the market economy where rice was concerned. One consequence was that Japan, South Korea, Taiwan, and other East Asian countries were essentially self-sufficient in rice, as supply management policy encouraged increased production because subsidies through price supports were generally based on volume produced. Consequently, in these countries, rice farmers saw their incomes rise. This is largely a function of the US food regime, which allowed and even encouraged such high levels of regulation.[15]

Second, although supply management policy aimed to prevent overproduction, it nevertheless tended to lead to surpluses. This was largely a consequence of the combination of price supports and production controls coupled with advances in agricultural technology in the middle of the twentieth century. Price supports were paid to farmers on the basis of volume produced. That is, farmers were given an artificially high price on all of the wheat or rice that they produced. Production controls, by contrast, were often centered on restricting land use. In the US, for example, maize farmers might be limited to growing corn on 70 percent of their farm. But there were generally few restrictions on the volume of maize that farmers could grow on that 70 percent of the farm. This effectively encouraged farmers to engage in intensive production to grow more on smaller proportions of land. Consequently, grain production and surpluses increased around the world as supply management policy spread.

We can see this dynamic clearly with wheat in the US and rice in Japan. In the 1950s, wheat production in the US increased steadily and surpluses mounted. The average yearly wheat surplus was about 28 MMT between 1954 and 1959, which meant that annual carry-over stocks ranged between 94 and 110 percent of annual wheat production. In fact, carry-over stocks of wheat "exceeded production in 1955, 1956, 1959, and 1961–1963."[16] As with wheat in the US and elsewhere, supply management policy did not reduce overproduction of rice in Japan. In fact, in the 1960s, price supports for rice created mounting surpluses that forced the Japanese government to increase production control measures substantially.[17]

Third, this food regime prompted changes in national diets through exports. At the outset of this chapter, we saw how diets in Japan and Colombia changed to include more wheat. In Japan, per capita rice consumption fell by 21 percent while per capita wheat consumption increased by 17 percent during the 1960s. Similarly, per capita maize consumption in Colombia fell by 24 percent and per capita wheat consumption rose by 12 percent. These "changes were driven in part by" US wheat exports and export subsidies. From 1954 to 1970, Japanese wheat imports increased from 1.8 MMT to 4.8 MMT, and its imports from the US increased from 1 MMT to 3 MMT. From 1960 to 1971, Colombia's wheat imports from the US increased from 0.13 MMT to 0.34 MMT. Importantly, wheat production in Colombia fell from 0.15 MMT in 1960 to just 0.06 MMT in 1971, suggesting that US wheat imports dampened domestic production in Colombia. This was also seen in South Korea, where subsidized wheat from the US "caused a steep fall in grain prices. As a result, farmers lost the incentive to produce and the agricultural production base began collapsing; some even set fire to agricultural products."[18] Thus, export subsidies helped to forge new markets for US wheat exports through shifts in national diets to include more wheat.

All of these effects of the US food regime ultimately served to undermine the regime itself. Taken together, the spread of supply management policy, the consequent overproduction of grains, and the use of export subsidies by many countries all led to greater competition between grains – either grains from different countries or different kinds of grains. For example, when Japan used export subsidies to alleviate its overproduction of rice, it was "forced to limit rice exports because of strong objections from commercial rice-exporting countries,"[19] that is, countries that did not subsidize exports. Two of the world's leading wheat-exporting nations, Canada and the US, also saw competition intensify as more countries subsidized wheat exports to compete for markets to dispose of surplus wheat. By 1980, at least 18 countries had adopted export subsidies to compete for markets and dispose of surplus grains.

These effects revealed an important contradiction in the US food regime that undermined its ability to function smoothly. The spread of supply management policy across the globe meant that countries not only adopted some combination of price supports and production controls, it also meant that countries adopted trade barriers to protect agriculture and the artificially high prices guaranteed by price supports. That is, the countries instituted high tariffs and other barriers to protect their domestic agriculture from competition by imports, which GATT allowed for agriculture. The more countries adopted supply management policy, then, the more restricted the grain trade became. Yet this increase in trade barriers arose at the same moment that countries saw their grain production increase, leading to an impetus to increase exports. To compete for markets, these countries had to adopt export subsidies, which more and more countries did. The US food regime presented subsidized exports as way to dispose of surplus grains, but this solution to overproduction began to break down.

This division and competition between grains, especially between wheat-producing nations, undermined the basic tenet of the US food regime: cooperation and coordination. Yet this was not the only central conflict between grains in this food regime. A division between food grains and feed grains also loomed large. Briefly put, feed grains producers were less supportive of supply management policy because of a substantial and steady increase in global meat production and consumption, which created growing demand for feed grains. Particularly in the US, organizations representing maize and soybean producers expressed opposition to supply management policy, especially production controls, as early as 1947. They did not have the political power to substantially change US agricultural policy, however, until after the 1990s.[20] Over the next 40 years, as Chapter 3 discusses, a search for new markets brought a variety of economic and political conflicts.

CHAPTER THREE

The Search for New Markets

On January 1, 1994, a peasant uprising occurred in Chiapas, Mexico. The rebels in this southern Mexican state were primarily indigenous Maya Indians, many or most of whom were subsistence farmers. Led by the Zapatista Army of National Liberation (EZLN), this rebellion aimed to confront a number of issues: the marginalization of the indigenous population, recent changes to the Mexican Constitution and national policies that undermined these people's land rights, and the neoliberal policies embodied in the North American Free Trade Agreement (NAFTA). The Chiapas rebellion began with the EZLN occupying a handful of cities in Chiapas, including San Cristóbal de Las Casas, Las Margaritas, Altamirano, and Ocosingo. The EZLN also took the former governor of Chiapas, Absalón Domínguez, as a prisoner of war. Through the First Declaration of the Lacandon Jungle, the EZLN declared war against the Mexican government and military, demanding liberty, justice, and democracy for all Mexicans.

In response, the federal government in Mexico sent in troops to put down the rebellion. This led to 12 days of fighting between the EZLN and the Mexican military. Then a cease-fire was called, and a long process of peace negotiations followed. This process brought global attention to the conflict and the Zapatistas, as well as to the cause of peasants and indigenous peoples around the world. In the years following the peace negotiations, however, the violence persisted as tensions continued to simmer and sometimes erupt between

EZLN rebels and para-military supporters of the Mexican government.

What does the geopolitics of grains have to do with this rebellion? Everything. The armed rebellion by indigenous peasants began on the day that NAFTA went into effect. In the US, political opposition to NAFTA centered on fears that industrial jobs would move south to Mexico, expanding the population of maquiladoras already dotting the Mexican–US border. Most people in the US knew little about the implications that NAFTA held for agriculture in Mexico – or for US agriculture, for that matter. The peasants in Chiapas, by contrast, saw clearly what NAFTA meant for their livelihoods, traditions, and communities. In 1992, as a precondition for Mexico entering NAFTA, the Mexican Constitution was modified to allow communal lands, ejidos, to become privatized. The ejidos were lands that indigenous peasants had long had traditional access to for subsistence agriculture. Thus, allowing the ejidos to be privately owned was a fundamental change that undermined the basic right to land that indigenous communities had according to Mexican law since 1934.

What prompted these changes in Mexican land tenure and agricultural policy? NAFTA played a central role. While much of the US public opposed or was at least concerned about NAFTA, farm organizations representing maize and soybean producers favored the free trade agreement. Mexico had long protected its maize producers from import competition, especially from the US, but NAFTA promised to open the Mexican market to US maize and soybeans. The Chiapas rebellion, then, was an armed uprising by peasant farmers fighting against changes in Mexican agricultural policy (e.g., ending subsidies for maize farmers) and land tenure brought about by NAFTA, which was supported by US maize farmers. It was a violent political conflict "caused in part by US" maize growers looking to get into the Mexican market.

So, how did it get to this point of such conflict between grains, especially given the context of international cooperation during the US food regime? Part of the answer lies in the search for new markets for grains beginning in the last quarter of the twentieth century. After the collapse of the US food regime in the 1970s, the global political-economic context of grains changed. It became more chaotic with greater volatility in prices. National agricultural policies began to change, threatening some farmers as competition to reshape the political landscape intensified. This chapter outlines how the search for new markets over the past 40 years unfolded as the previous organization of the world economy disappeared, leading to changes and competition among grain producers. It also highlights some of the political struggles that accompanied this search for new markets. Not all of the political struggles have been as dramatic or violent as the Chiapas rebellion, but there have been many important implications from the various political struggles over grains.

After the US Food Regime

The fall of the US food regime coincided with a fundamental shift in the world economy in general. From 1945 to 1975, the world economy saw a substantial degree of national and international regulation and coordination in a variety of economic and social issues – what some scholars have referred to as "embedded liberalism," which indicates the presence of a liberal market economy that is regulated in many sectors. During this period of US hegemony in the world economy, national governments and international organizations used a variety of regulations and policies to coordinate the world economy in most sectors, including finance, industry, the labor market, and food and agriculture. In addition, national governments provided workers and citizens with a variety of social protections from the vagaries of the market economy, including public pensions, medical care, poverty and income assistance, food and nutritional assistance, environmental regulations, and so on. All of these policies and regulations aimed to keep the market economy connected to – or embedded with – other social institutions in a way that helped to temper the extreme fluctuations of the market. This embedded liberalism, however, began to unravel by the 1970s, and there was a shift toward a more liberal world economy.

Liberalization in the World Economy
What does that mean, "a more liberal world economy"? Many fundamental changes occurred by the mid-1970s that reduced, weakened, or altogether eliminated many of the regulations and policies that made up embedded liberalism. One example of such a change can be seen in the financial sector in terms of currency exchange rates. Beginning in 1946, financial markets in the world economy were governed by the Bretton Woods Accord, which created a system of fixed (i.e., regulated) currencies. In 1971, the US moved away from its policy of holding the dollar exchange at 1/35th of an ounce of gold, so that the currency was no longer fixed. With the Smithsonian Agreement in 1973, most other countries also shifted away from fixed currencies. The result was a much more fluid and market-oriented currency system that was more vulnerable to market swings.

Another example of the liberal shift in the world economy can be seen in what scholars at the time called the "new international divisions of labor." Industrial production – for example in steel, automobiles, and consumer appliances – began to move out of the industrial belts in the US and Europe and into lower-wage regions and countries. This involved the spreading of components of production across the globe. The driving forces behind this new international division of labor included corporations seeking reduced labor costs, environmental regulations, taxes, business regulations, and so forth.

Along with fluctuating currency exchange rates and the greater mobility of industrial production, there were also sharp reductions in the barriers to cross-border capital flows. This meant that foreign investment capital could enter a country and invest heavily in real estate and push up rental prices, for example, and then withdraw from the country quickly with the result being a collapse in prices. This stands in contrast to previous national regulations that required a certain period of time over which investments had to occur or that limited foreign investments in various ways. This increased mobility for capital contributed to the East Asian financial crisis in 1997.

Finally, a number of social protections came under attack, including public pensions, union rights, and poverty assistance. During this period, the welfare state experienced a contraction. Union density decreased in many countries beginning in the 1970s. At the same time, expenditures decreased and eligibility narrowed for social support programs in many countries. This was true, as we will see in more detail shortly, of support for farmers as well. Thus, the aspects of embedded liberalism that helped to protect individuals and workers from the vagaries of the market were weakened, in some cases substantially.

Another change also portended a more liberal world economy: the decline of communism in Eastern Europe and the Soviet Union, in conjunction with the rise of markets in China. The decline of communism opened markets for grains that had previously been extensively regulated or even closed off. The fall of communism also altered the distribution of some wheat export markets. As noted in Chapter 2, Canada had focused on exporting wheat to China and the Soviet Union. The fall of communism in the early 1990s and the opening of China to trade altered this pattern in wheat exports.

Beyond these shifts in the world economy, a number of crises also occurred in the 1970s that signaled the breakdown of both US hegemony and embedded liberalism. First, the oil crisis of 1973 saw oil prices skyrocket from about US$3 a barrel to US$12. Supplies were limited, and long lines of cars became common sights at gas stations. Given oil's central place as a source for energy and industrial production, the spike in prices had a number of disruptive economic and political consequences. Second, a food crisis also struck the world economy between 1972 and 1974, sending food prices to historic levels. Wheat prices rose from an annual average of US$69 per MMT in 1972 to US$179 in 1974 – an increase of 160 percent. Third, a military crisis also came to a head in the early 1970s: the US withdrew from Vietnam in 1975, but direct US military involvement ended in 1973 when Congress passed the Case–Church Amendment. Fourth and finally, poorer countries around the world experienced a debt crisis. For some countries, this was partly a function of their recent emergence from being colonies. Most of Africa and parts of Asia and the Middle East became independent countries between about 1955 and 1965. These new nations required some financial assistance, which came from the World Bank and the International Monetary Fund (IMF). But new nations were not alone in receiving loans and expanding public debt. Other countries in Latin America and elsewhere also saw an expansion in public debt. This growing debt became a problem when inflation and interest rates rose quickly at the same time as the world economy entered its most significant recession since the 1930s. As a consequence, national incomes and economic growth rates declined, making it more difficult for many countries to meet loan payments – leading to a debt crisis. The IMF made structural adjustment loans available to many countries. These loans enabled countries to meet their debt obligations but also required significant cuts in public spending and sometimes expansive privatization. One consequence of these loans was a significant reduction in agriculture, in terms of subsidies, research, and so forth. More broadly, though, these crises signaled a significant change.

In short, then, the world economy entered a moment of historic and fundamental change in the 1970s. The embedded liberalism and national regulations that undergirded US hegemony for about 25 years were dismantled. Political, economic, and food crises struck, signaling a break with the past. International coordination in the world economy unraveled. The shift toward a more liberal world economy continued for the next few decades and into the twenty-first century. Within this context, supply management policy and coordination in world markets for grains began to unravel and shift.

Agriculture and Liberalization

Agriculture, particularly grains, followed this same general historical trajectory between 1970 and 2010. The shift for grains, and agriculture more generally, can be traced through several trends and events: the breakdown of international commodity agreements, changes in national agricultural policies, the incorporation of agriculture into GATT, the creation of the WTO, and the spread of bilateral and regional free trade agreements.

The first step on this path was the breakdown and reconfiguration of the IWA and other international commodity agreements. As discussed in Chapter 2, the IWA worked to coordinate and regulate wheat prices, production, and trade from 1949 to 1970. During this time the IWA was successful at creating a more stable world market for wheat. In 1970, however, talks to renew the IWA ran into problems, as the US and Canada disagreed over market shares and other issues. From that time forward, the IWA no longer exerted the same regulatory influence over prices, production, and trade. Instead, the focus of the agreement began to shift toward marketing issues and away from regulation. Given wheat's central position in the US food regime, the breakdown and reconfiguration of the IWA in the early 1970s was a historic moment. For wheat producers, this began a period of greater instability in markets, prices, national policies, and production. International agreements for other commodities, including coffee and cocoa, also broke down and became less far reaching in their regulatory influence and ability to coordinate markets. By the late 1990s, these commodity agreements came to focus more squarely on marketing issues and support rather than on stabilizing prices or regulating production or trade. The overarching mechanism for coordinating and regulating the world wheat market was, therefore, dismantled.

In the 1980s, there was a growing push to incorporate agriculture into GATT. International tensions and disputes over agricultural trade increased as competition for markets intensified and agricultural policies expanded. Countries often turned to GATT institutions to help resolve such disputes. The FAO states that, "60 percent of all trade disputes submitted to the GATT dispute settlement process between 1980 and 1990 were concerned with agriculture."[1] Through most of the mid-twentieth century, agriculture's exemption from GATT liberalization was left largely unchallenged in any meaningful way. Critics of protections and regulations for agriculture had long called for the end of supply management, but there was little force behind such positions until the 1980s. With the Uruguay Round of GATT talks, which began in 1987, discussions were had about pushing agriculture to liberalize. This liberalization focused on increasing import access by reducing trade barriers, reducing domestic support programs for agriculture, and reducing export subsidies.

The incorporation of agriculture into GATT was not the only example of expanding liberalization through trade agreements. A variety of bilateral and regional free trade agreements also aimed to weaken regulations on agriculture. NAFTA serves as one primary example. Importantly, this free trade agreement was driven in part by divisions between maize and wheat. In the US, wheat producers opposed NAFTA as they worried about competition from Canadian wheat. US maize producers, by contrast, favored NAFTA as they saw it as an opportunity to enter the Mexican market. Some Mexican maize producers, as we have seen, strongly and violently opposed NAFTA. Beyond NAFTA, regional free trade agreements have proliferated with amazing frequency over the past 30 years or so, and especially in the past 15 years. There have been even more bilateral free trade agreements during this period. Importantly, these regional and bilateral free trade agreements generally have an agricultural component, meaning that they have liberalized agriculture.

At about the same time that international commodity agreements were weakened, national policies of supply management began also to weaken. Even the US shifted its agricultural policy in a way that also weakened supply management. In 1973, the US reduced price supports, suspended production controls, and shifted from food aid to commercial exports. Maize producers continued to oppose supply management, but the world-economic context of greater demand for wheat in the early 1970s also led US wheat producers to look more favorably or acceptingly on weakening price supports and production controls. Many other countries also relaxed their policies of supply management. For example, Japan saw some retrenchment in its agricultural policy at about the same time as the US: "Between 1982 and 1991, the [Japanese] Ministry of Agriculture budget declined by 26 percent . . . [and] expenditures for food control (mostly rice supports) . . . declined in real terms by 68 percent."[2] Supply management policy contracted for both rice and wheat during this time.

Some other countries, by contrast, actually expanded supply management policy for a brief time during the 1970s, when others were moving away from supply management policy. South Korea, in particular, expanded its use of price supports for rice in response to the US shifting from food aid to (more expensive) commercial exports. South Korean agricultural policy began to encourage increased rice production, partly through higher prices and also through the use of Green Revolution technologies. Similarly, in the 1970s, Saudi Arabia increased price supports with the intent of increasing wheat production. In the coming decades, however, even these countries began to roll back supply management policy, reducing price supports and production controls.

Nevertheless, this retrenchment of supply management policy continued through the beginning of the twenty-first century. Perhaps most notably, the Federal Agriculture Improvement and Reform (FAIR) Act essentially ended supply management policy in the US in 1996. First, price supports were fundamentally changed by the FAIR Act, which replaced income payments tied to market prices (i.e., price supports) with direct payments that were decoupled from prices. Even more importantly, though, production controls were eliminated. Without production controls, the US ended its goal of managing the supply of agricultural commodities, as it had for most of the twentieth century. This shift in US agricultural policy away from supply management policy coincided closely in time with NAFTA, the incorporation of agriculture into GATT, and the creation of the WTO.

Other countries were likewise influenced by such changes in the world economy in the 1990s. For example, US rice producers filed a complaint with the US government against Japan's rice import policy. The US government then took the complaint to the Uruguay Round talks. In 1994, the Japanese government enacted amendments to the Rice Control Act that "deregulated portions of the domestic rice market (it [became] possible for small shopkeepers to sell rice), but the government [continued to operate] a licensing system and exercises control over access to the wholesale rice market."[3] Therefore, just as the supply management policy contracted in the US in the 1990s, it did so in Japan, as well as other countries. Despite idiosyncratic differences in how national agricultural policies changed, then, the pace of liberalization in agriculture was remarkably similar across the world economy.

All of this – the end of the IWA, the retrenchment of national policies of supply management, the incorporation of agriculture into GATT, and the creation of the WTO and its Agreement on Agriculture – resulted in a world-economic context that was quite distinct from that of the US food regime.

The Search for New Markets and Economic Conflict in Agriculture

The liberalization of the world economy has been intimately tied to the search for new markets for grains and to shifts in patterns in the production, trade, and consumption of grains. On the one hand, the origins of this fundamental shift are linked to the divisions between grains, as we have seen with the pursuit of greater liberalization through much of the twentieth century by feed grain producers, particularly in the US. On the other hand, this liberalization led to and shaped new markets for both food grains and feed grains. Most importantly, however, these new markets did not mean the end of competition among grain producers. If anything, the emergence of new markets and reorganization of the world economy brought intensified competition to grain markets. We can see this intensified competition in three examples:

the wheat subsidy war between the US and Europe in the 1980s, the push to bring agriculture into GATT trade talks, and the expansion of the livestock sector. Each of these examples entails political and economic struggles between grains directly connected to the reorganization of markets that came with the liberalization of the world economy.

Wheat Subsidy War: Europe versus the US
Perhaps the clearest example of conflicts emerging from the geopolitics of grains and the search for new markets can be found in the subsidy war over wheat between Europe and the US during the 1980s. This subsidy war centered on the use of export subsidies as a tool to capture greater shares of the world wheat market. Importantly, this conflict over wheat pushed forward the liberalization in agriculture, more generally. That is, this political conflict played a central role in the liberalization of the world economy.

The deep roots of this conflict can be found in the adoption of supply management policy. An important consequence of this policy, as seen in the previous chapter, was increased production and expanding agricultural surpluses. For Europe, this consequence emerged after the adoption of the Common Agricultural Policy (CAP): beginning in the 1960s, wheat production increased and, consequently, so did wheat exports as Europe sought an outlet for its surplus wheat. Figure 3.1 shows trends in European wheat production and exports. Wheat production in Europe increased under CAP from 35 MMT in 1960 to 50 MMT in 1975, reaching 90 MMT in 1984. The CAP price supports and increased use of technology (e.g., machinery, chemical fertilizers) were the primary basis of this increase in production.

Increased production in grains led to two important outcomes. First, Europe restricted imports of feed grains, including soybeans, in the early 1980s. These imports had

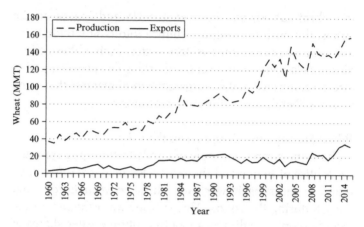

Figure 3.1. European Wheat Production and Exports, 1960–2015.
Source: Foreign Agricultural Service, USDA, "PS&D Online Database."

come primarily from the US, which "responded in 1982 by trying to break into a traditional European wheat market – Egypt – by offering a cut-rate price for flour. When the European Community (EC) sold butter in traditional US markets at below commercial prices, the United States retaliated by withdrawing from the International Dairy Agreement (which set minimum world prices for dairy) so it could sell its dairy surpluses on world markets at low prices."[4] The closing off of the European market to US feed grains helped to kick start trade battles with the US.

Second, Europe expanded its grain exports, which then frequently put it in competition with the US for markets around the world. European wheat exports increased over the 1980s, from 5 MMT in 1977 to 23 MMT in 1992. This created greater competition in the world wheat market and led to a trade subsidy battle between the US and Europe, as seen in Figure 3.2. The US share of world wheat exports dropped from 48 percent in 1981 to 29 percent in 1985. One important factor in

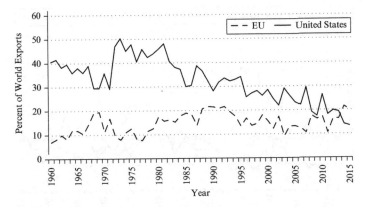

Figure 3.2. European and US Wheat Exports as a Percent of World Exports, 1960–2015.

Source: Foreign Agricultural Service, USDA, "PS&D Online Database."

this change in the world wheat market was the emergence of Europe as a wheat exporter. From 1965 to 1979, Europe had been a net importer of wheat. But Europe became a net exporter of wheat beginning in 1980. France was the primary force behind this shift, as wheat production in France increased significantly beginning in the 1960s, from 9.5 MMT in 1961 to 28 MMT in 1985. In the early 1990s, wheat production in France reached about 33 MMT, and it was almost 40 MMT per year by 2000. The most significant and sustained increase in French wheat production came between 1975 and 1991, when it increased from 15 MMT to 33 MMT. In the early 1990s, however, world demand for grain was relatively stable while world grain production was relatively high. Furthermore, the increased competition in the world wheat market was not simply between the US and Europe. As Figure 3.3 shows, the world wheat market became increasingly competitive after 1975. Consequently, the European Community had to use export subsidies to find markets for its surplus grain – not

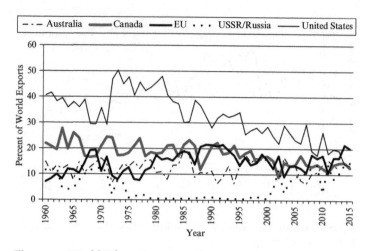

Figure 3.3. World Wheat Exports, 1960–2015.
Source: Foreign Agricultural Service, USDA, "PS&D Online Database."

unlike the US had to do after the Second World War during the early stages of the US food regime. One source of markets for this surplus wheat was to use it as animal feed. The other source for markets was through trade – that is, capturing US markets by using export subsidies.

In response, the US created the Export Enhancement Program (EEP) in 1985. This program expanded export subsidies for wheat, and for the next five years PL 480, the EEP, or similar programs subsidized at least two-thirds of US wheat exports. From 1977 to 1984, the US subsidized about 25 percent of its wheat exports each year, on average. Between 1985 and 1993, it subsidized about 72 percent of its wheat exports. Europe and the US competed for wheat markets in Asia, Eastern Europe, North Africa, and elsewhere by expanding their use of export subsidies. Initially, in the 1980s, the competition over markets focused on northern Africa and the Middle East, where the US and EC countered one another's subsidies with ever larger subsidies. In 1985, the average EC subsidy per metric ton increased from less than US$38 to more than US$60, more than US$100 in 1986, and more than US$130 in 1987. These were the years of the most intense competition for markets. From 1986 to 1995, export subsidies were used for no less than 67 percent of US exports and as much as 80 percent of US exports in 1987. During this period, the US and the EC increased wheat exports to China, North Africa, and the Soviet Union.

This competition led to lower wheat prices, which not only hurt US and European wheat farmers but also hurt farmers of traditional grains in importing countries. For example, grain, millet, and cassava farmers in northern Africa could not compete effectively with heavily subsidized grain imports from the US and Europe. The subsidized grain imports also depressed grain prices in the region. In addition, the increasing subsidies by the US and Europe lowered world prices for grains, thereby undermining the incomes of grain farmers around the world – particularly those grain farmers in countries without the resources to offer subsidies. And finally, other grain-exporting nations had to subsidize their exports to compete. For example, Canada substantially enlarged its wheat exports in 1987 in response to the US–EC competition for markets.

In Europe, one primary consequence of this wheat subsidy war was the creation of political schisms between key member nations, primarily France, Germany, and the UK. France favored subsidizing exports at high levels to maintain shares of world markets, but the growing EC expenditures on CAP increasingly led Germany and the UK, which were not major grain exporters, to pay more to provide such subsidies. Nonetheless, the agricultural sector in Germany was large enough that it prompted a German–France coalition to maintain CAP subsidies, including on exports, despite British opposition. These subsidies continued to be a source of division globally and soon contributed to a shift in the global trading system.

The Battle to Put Agriculture into GATT

In the wake of this competition for grain markets, there emerged a push to incorporate agriculture into GATT, which serves as yet another example of increased competition between grains as nations and producers sought to establish new markets. In the 1980s, "this push was initiated in part by several" grain-exporting countries, led by Australia, Brazil, and Canada. Known as the Cairns Group, these countries pushed for reductions in trade barriers for grains in the world economy. The position of the Cairns Group was tied directly to the wheat trade war between the US and Europe. Nations in the Cairns Group did not have the budgets to spend on export subsidies to the same extent as seen in the US and Europe. Consequently, these wheat-exporting nations found their share of world markets shrinking. Here again, the fall of the US food regime and the liberalization of the world economy pitted grain producers against one another.

This incorporation of agriculture into GATT, which was a fundamental shift in world trade policy, was rooted in the geopolitics of grains, especially wheat. This can be seen in various forces behind the push to include agriculture in the Agreement. First, several countries that exported grains and other agricultural commodities formed the Cairns Group in 1986: Argentina, Australia, Brazil, Canada, Indonesia, Malaysia, New Zealand, Pakistan, Peru, the Philippines, South Africa, Thailand, and Uruguay. This coalition pushed for liberalization in agricultural trade through substantial reductions in tariffs, the elimination of trade-distorting domestic subsidies, and the elimination of export subsidies. As net exporters of agricultural commodities, these countries generally shared a common interest in liberalizing agricultural trade. The Cairns Group had two particular targets. On the one hand, the Cairns Group took aim at tariff barriers that accompanied supply management, particularly in the US and Europe. Not only did supply management policy in the US and Europe limit the access the Cairns members had to North American and European markets, but these policies also led to grain surpluses that were shipped abroad using export subsidies. This led to the other target of the Cairns Group. They sought to reduce or eliminate export subsidies, particularly for wheat, in the US and Europe. Many countries in the Cairns Group exported grains but could not compete with subsidized exports from the US or Europe. Foreshadowing conflicts to come in the early twenty-first century, the Cairns Group pursued negotiations in GATT until agriculture was included. The incorporation of agriculture, therefore, became a necessary component of GATT moving forward.

Second and somewhat paradoxically, the US also began to push for the incorporation of agriculture into GATT. The Reagan administration helped to lead this push, which also included agrifood corporations such as Archer Daniels Midland and Cargill. Part of the impetus behind the US position was the trade war with Europe over wheat subsidies. While the US had been the primary original advocate for exempting agriculture from GATT's liberalizing drive, the wheat subsidy war with Europe pushed the US to the forefront of efforts to incorporate agriculture into GATT in the early 1980s.

Pushed by these disparate forces – the Cairns Group, the US, and agrifood corporations, among others – the Uruguay Round of GATT talks began in 1987. The primary debate, however, occurred between the US and Europe, as the former advocated for greater liberalization in agricultural trade and aimed to reduce the protection and support enjoyed by producers in Europe under the CAP. Europe, by contrast, was much less interested in extending liberalization in agriculture but, nevertheless, wanted to reach a compromise, that could be codified in GATT, to reduce the possibility of future trade disputes with the US.

Agriculture was finally included in GATT through the Blair House Accord of 1992, which made several proposals, including reducing the volume of subsidized wheat exports by 21 percent, establishing guidelines to further reduce export subsidies, and reducing domestic agricultural support programs (e.g., price supports). These elements of the Blair House Accord were the basis on which the US and EC agreed to liberalize agriculture. The Uruguay Round talks ended in 1993 and included agriculture for the first time within the framework of GATT, thereby subjecting agriculture to GATT disciplines.

This final round of GATT resulted in the creation of the World Trade Organization (WTO) in 1995. The WTO replaced GATT as the location of settlement for disputes regarding trade regulations as well as the locus for the development of new trade agreements and regulations in the world economy. The primary aim of the WTO is to further liberalize the world economy, continuing the direction set by GATT. The Uruguay Round of GATT included the development of the WTO Agreement on Agriculture (AoA), which also took effect in 1995. The AoA has three central foci: domestic support, market access, and export subsidies. The AoA aims to further liberalize agriculture in each of these areas.

First, regarding domestic support, the AoA created a system of three "boxes" to characterize different types of income support for farmers. Amber box supports have ties to production levels, such as price supports, and encourage excessive production and, thereby, distort trade. Blue box supports have direct ties to production but also limit production by imposing production quotas or requiring land set-asides. Blue box supports are understood in WTO rules to be "partially decoupled" from production and are not subject to WTO reduction commitments. Direct payments are an example of blue box supports. Green box supports are understood to cause minimal trade distortions, at most, and are not subject to WTO reduction commitments. Subsidies that are decoupled, or independent of, prices or production are the central example of green box supports. These supports can also require that no production occur, such as in land set-aside programs. The AoA set goals for reducing supports in each of these categories.

Second, the AoA focuses on market access, which means reducing tariffs on agricultural imports. Access to agricultural markets in core countries was a key issue for peripheral countries. The 1995 AoA required core countries to reduce tariffs by 36 percent over six years, and the tariff for any given commodity had to be reduced by at least 15 percent during that time. It also required peripheral countries to reduce tariffs by 24 percent over ten years, and the tariff for any given commodity had to be reduced no less than 10 percent during that time. On this issue of market access, the EU and Japan tended to side with smaller tariff reductions while the US and the Cairns Group favored greater tariff reductions.

Third, the 1995 AoA called for reductions in export subsidies, demanding reductions of at least 36 percent by value or by at least 21 percent by volume over the six years in core countries. The AoA also required developing countries to reduce export subsidies by 14 percent by volume and 24 percent by value over ten years. Currently, however, export subsidies tied directly to the volume of exports are prohibited by the WTO. The AoA, then, aimed to liberalize agriculture in the world economy in a number of ways.

Yet after the creation of the WTO in 1995, resistance to liberalizing agriculture intensified and was led by farmers, farm organizations, and governments from poorer countries.

Among the nations taking a prominent position against the WTO's Agreement on Agriculture was South Korea, which viewed the AoA as a threat to its agricultural policy supporting rice farmers. This resistance led several consecutive WTO ministerial meetings to break down. In 2003, for example, the WTO ministerial meetings were in Cancun, Mexico. At the start of the meeting on September 10, Kun Hai Lee, a South Korean farmer and activist, committed ritual suicide to protest the WTO's efforts to liberalize agriculture. The meeting was then unraveled by thousands of protesters in the streets, in part led by La Via Campesina, an international organization working for the rights of peasants and small farmers around the world, while the G23 – a group of developing nations, led by Brazil, China, India, and South Africa – provided formal resistance to the WTO in the meeting rooms. These small grain farmers and peasants, as well as the representatives from their national governments, effectively blocked attempts to liberalize agriculture. By looking at the ministerial meetings, then, we can see an ongoing struggle over the rules governing agriculture, particularly grains, in the world economy.

Importantly, the liberalization of agriculture in the world economy has highlighted three economic conflicts between grains. First, the US and Europe battled over wheat markets and the use of export subsidies. This conflict carried over into the GATT talks and the creation of the WTO. Second, grain-exporting nations formed the Cairns Group as a means to confront the US and especially Europe on the issue of export subsidies. And third, the G23 and international organizations of peasants and small grain farmers blocked the expansion and development of liberalization by the WTO. In addition to these battles, which have largely been between food grains, the push for liberalization also involved a division between food grains and feed grains.

Meat Consumption and Competition between Grains
The expanding global meat industry provides the final example of political and economic struggles directly connected to the reorganization of markets that came with the liberalization of the world economy. At the end of Chapter 2, we briefly saw how the shift in political power toward feed grains in the US contributed to the decline of supply management policy and the US food regime. The liberalization of the world economy continued the split between food grains and feed grains, and it also saw another split emerge regarding biofuels.

The basis of the competition between food grain and feed grain producers has been tied to the global expansion of meat production and consumption. Feed grain producers – primarily maize and soybean farmers, especially in the core of the world economy – pushed for the expansion of free trade and continued to fight against many national policies regulating agriculture. By contrast, many food grain farmers around the world have tended to favor national regulations in the form of price supports, production controls, or export subsidies. This increase in meat production and consumption set up a familiar split between food grains and feed grains. Wheat farmers in the US, Europe, and other countries continued to face a relatively competitive international market, and therefore continued to favor some elements of supply management policy. Rice producers likewise continued to favor supply management since they focused little on exports. Farmers growing maize for food also tended to favor supply management. By contrast, feed grain producers – both maize and soybean producers – tended to oppose supply management policy because of the promise of expanding markets as meat production increased around the globe.

Figure 3.4 shows the increase in global meat consumption. From 1975 to 2000, the total meat consumption in the world increased from 26 kg per capita to 35 kg per capita. During the

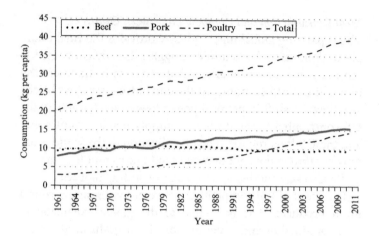

Figure 3.4. Global per Capita Meat Consumption, 1961–2011.

Source: Food and Agriculture Organization, United Nations, "FAOSTAT."

same period, the world's population increased from 4 billion people to 6 billion. So at the same time that the world's population increased by about 50 percent, per capita meat consumption also increased by about 35 percent. Of course, each of these trends has continued to increase since 2000. In 2011, about 6.9 billion people consumed an average of 39 kg of meat per capita.

Behind this increase in world meat consumption, of course, is a significant increase in meat production. Figure 3.5 shows world meat production from 1960 to 2015. In 1970, there were about 67 MMT of meat produced. By 1995, world meat production had more than doubled, reaching about 164 MMT. Over that 26-year span, world meat production increased by an average of about 3.7 MMT per year. Since 1995, the expansion of livestock production has been even faster. In 2015, world meat production reached 258 MMT. Between 1995 and 2015, the average annual increase in meat production

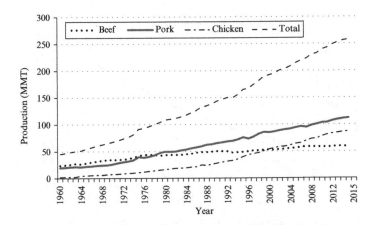

Figure 3.5. World Meat Production, 1960–2015.
Source: Foreign Agricultural Service, USDA, "PS&D Online Database."

was 4.5 MMT. In many ways, this more clearly captures the growth in meat consumption, which rested on an increasing number of animals being raised, fed, and slaughtered for human consumption.

To put it in terms of animals slaughtered each year is perhaps even more illustrative. As Figure 3.6 shows, the number of cows slaughtered for meat increased between 1961 and 2013, but the rate of increase slowed after about 1975. In 1961, about 172 million cows were slaughtered for meat, reaching 246 million cows in 1985 and 296 million in 2010. The number of pigs and chickens slaughtered for meat, by contrast, increased dramatically over this period. The period began with 376 million pigs slaughtered, and 815 million pigs were slaughtered in 1985. In 1995, more than 1 billion pigs were slaughtered, and the number of pigs killed continued to increase rapidly, reaching 1.4 billion in 2013. The increase in the number of chickens killed for meat was even more dramatic, and the total number dwarfed the number of cows

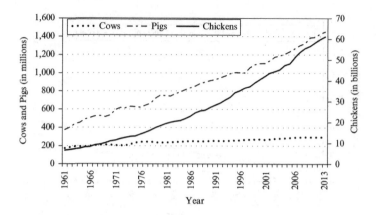

Figure 3.6. World Meat Production: Number of Animals Slaughtered, 1961–2013.

Source: Food and Agriculture Organization, United Nations, "FAOSTAT."

or pigs slaughtered. In 1961, a total of 6.1 billion chickens were slaughtered for meat. In 1985, the number of chickens killed that year reached almost 22 billion, and about 61 billion chickens were slaughtered for meat in 2013. Not only did the number of animals slaughtered for meat increase during this period, but the average size of the animals also increased – a result of selective breeding and the expansion of the industrial livestock sector.

Part of the expansion of global meat production is tied to the fall of communism, which also contributed to increase, or at least alter, competition. The end of the Cold War meant greater competition for those grain markets in China and Eastern Europe. Communist states made attempts to expand meat production "and consumption by relying at least in part on feed" grain imports from the West, especially the US. After the fall of communism in the early 1990s, the livestock industry grew in the former communist countries, both to expand domestic meat consumption but also to increase meat exports.

For example, Smithfield Farms – one of the largest pork pro-ducers in the world – expanded operations in Poland in 1999 and Romania in 2004. Smithfield brought factory farming to Eastern Europe, significantly increasing pork production in these countries.

This expansion in the meat industry required a great many resources in terms of animal lives, land, water, and grains. While world rice and wheat production more than tripled between 1960 and 2015 – rice production increased from 150 MMT to 470 MMT, and wheat production increased from 233 MMT to 735 MMT – and certainly, these are very impressive increases in food grains production, world produc-tion of feed rose at least as much. World maize production also increased more than threefold, from about 299 MMT in 1960 to 967 MMT in 2015. World soybean production, how-ever, increased more than tenfold, from just 29 MMT in 1964 to 319 MMT in 2015. For both maize and soybeans, world production accelerated faster beginning around 2000. The expansion in global meat production has helped to fuel this dramatic increase in feed grain production.

It is important to recognize, though, that most of the world's maize farmers do not necessarily favor liberalization. This is due, to a significant extent, to how maize is used – for food or for feed. We have already seen how maize producers in Mexico revolted against the liberalization of agriculture through NAFTA. Again, these maize farmers were producing maize as a food grain. Nonetheless, even in Latin America, the production of feed grains has increased. Soybean production has increased in the region, as have its soybean exports to the EU and Asia. Prior to 1975, there were few soybean exports from South America – less than 1 MMT per year. Annual soy-bean exports from the region averaged about 5 MMT by 1985 and reached 11 MMT in 1996. A more significant jump in exports occurred in about 2000 and then 2009, when annual soybean exports reached 25 MMT and 47 MMT, respectively. This expansion in soybean production and exports from South America has a clear link to the increase in global meat consumption and production. Furthermore, farmers participating in such expansions in feed grains likely share similar economic interests and policy preferences with feed grain producers in the core of the world economy (i.e., in favor of liberalization) rather than with those farmers of maize for food in the same region.

In addition to the division between food grains and feed grains, a new split in grains has recently emerged in relation to feed grains and meat consumption. This new split is primarily a function of a new use of maize: biofuels. Particularly in the US, maize has come to be used increasingly as ethanol. In the middle of the twentieth century, most of the maize produced in the US was used for feed for livestock. The increased maize production from 1945 to 1990 was crucial to the expansion of meat production and consumption during this same period. In the early 2000s, a key shift occurred in which more maize that otherwise would have gone into feed grains has gone into biofuels production. Joseph Baines finds that the ethanol boom in the 2000s increased "the earnings of the Agro-Trader nexus and corn growers while reducing the earnings of the Animal Processor nexus and livestock farmers."[5] This represents a potentially new and important division among grains, feed grains in particular. Three important agrifood corporations led the Agro-Trader nexus and its support of biofuels production: ADM, Monsanto, and DuPont. As Chapter 5 discusses, Monsanto and DuPont are the leading GE seed companies, which gave them a particular interest in facilitating the expansion of maize production. And more generally, the expansion in biofuels represents one more way that the demand for feed grains has expanded, allowing for the pursuit of continued expanding production

– and continued support of liberalization in the world economy.

We have now seen how divisions between grains – especially between food grains and feed grains – have contributed to the emergence of economic and political conflicts. As with the case of the Chiapas rebellion, sometimes these conflicts erupt into violence. The competition over access to markets – as seen in the wheat subsidy war between the US and Europe, as well as between the Cairns Group and the US and EU – created sharp tensions and also helped to drive the direction of the food regime toward liberalization. Finally, the divisions between feed grains and food grains contributed to conflicts over the liberalization of agriculture, which the former favored while the latter did not. The divisions were in part rooted in competition within the world grain markets, as well as the potential for new export markets.

This same division and potential conflict between food grains and feed grains, based on expanding demand for the latter, has also been a contributing factor to one of the most pressing and long-term issues that people have faced: adequate access to nutritious food. World hunger and food security, as the next chapter discusses, are connected to the liberalization of agriculture, as well as divisions between food grains and feed grains.

CHAPTER FOUR

Feed Grains, Food Grains, and World Hunger

In 2007, food riots broke out in West Bengal, India, as poor rural communities resisted corruption in the food rationing system. As described in *Time* magazine in February 2008, "Indian protesters burned hundreds of food-ration stores in West Bengal last October, accusing the owners of selling government-subsidized food on the lucrative black market."[1] Consequently, three food distributors killed themselves, and protesters set fire to the home of another food distributor and to the ruling party offices. These food riots took place in several locations across this western Indian state, and resulted in police killing two protesters and more than 300 protesters being injured. Then in 2008, additional food riots erupted after flooding had displaced more than 2 million people from their homes and food appeared to be in short supply. Again, protesters attacked food distributors, government officials, and local politicians as they demanded access to food.[2]

Perhaps as notable as the food protests and riots themselves were the responses of the Indian government to both the demands of protesters and the emerging chaos in the market during the global food crisis of 2008. First, the Indian government imposed a ban on the export of non-basmati rice and an export tax on basmati rice. Second, the government increased wheat subsidies to try to address rising wheat prices. Third, the government imposed a ban on maize exports. Finally, in 2013, the Indian government passed the National Food Security Act, which expanded some government programs already in existence and created several new ones: a midday meal program, child development services, general grain subsidies through the Public Distribution System, and maternity entitlements. The result is that approximately two-thirds of the country's population receives some food aid from the government.

India was by no means the only country to experience unrest during the global food crisis: in 2007 and 2008, food riots struck in more than 30 countries, including Bangladesh, Burkina Faso, Cameroon, Egypt, Haiti, Indonesia, Mexico, Pakistan, Senegal, Uzbekistan, and Yemen, among numerous others. Another wave of food riots struck again in 2010 and 2011, helping to give rise to the "Arab Spring" in North Africa and the Middle East. As in 2008, these protests and riots occurred in the context of rising global food prices. Several years prior to these protests and increased food prices, there was global agreement on concrete goals to reduce world hunger and food insecurity. More than ten years earlier, in 1996, the World Food Summit, convened by the FAO, established the goal to reduce the number of people suffering from hunger in the world by half by the year 2015. And in 2000, the United Nations set Millennium Development Goals to reduce the percent of the world's population suffering from hunger by half.[3] Therefore, much global attention has been focused on the issues of world hunger and food security since the mid-1990s. Yet in 2007, chaos began to beset world agricultural markets and led to rising hunger, greater food insecurity, and less political stability – such as seen in the "Ration Riots" in India.[4]

Why did grain prices rise, leading to concerns about food supply in India and elsewhere? The answer is connected to trends in the world economy discussed in the previous chapter, most notably a shift toward liberal policies governing grains. The geopolitics of grains has also influenced patterns in world hunger and food security, just as grains shaped the food regime and the world economy. This chapter examines various dimensions of the global food crisis in 2008: the role of markets and national policies in rising rice prices, the influence of biofuels policy, the financialization of agriculture, and finally the effects of the food crisis in the US and the Middle East. Then the chapter explores the long-term issue of food security and how it relates to grain markets, particularly the grain trade. Here we will begin by looking at food security in South Asia, a region of the world that has had chronic food security issues. Next we will explore the case of quinoa and return to the effects of meat production. The connection between hunger and world grain markets is nothing new, of course. So, our examination of how the geopolitics of grains relates to hunger begins by looking at various instances in history that reveal these dynamics. First, however, we turn to the concepts of world hunger and food security.

World Hunger and Food Security

World hunger refers to the portion of the population suffering from undernourishment, or insufficient caloric intake. While seemingly straightforward, measuring world hunger can be complicated. In 2012, the FAO introduced a new measure to estimate world hunger: the "prevalence of undernourishment." Using this measure, the FAO estimates that about 795 million people, or about 11 percent of the world's population, suffered from hunger in 2015. Notably, this relatively new measure of world hunger results in lower estimates than did the previous method. Some alternative measures of world hunger put the estimate at about 1 billion people. The difference rests on who is defined as hungry in terms of the number of calories consumed and the length of time they have been deprived of adequate calorie levels. Given these different measures, it may be more useful to state the amount of world hunger as ranging between about 795 million and 1 billion people, or about 11–13 percent of the world's population.[5]

Food security is another way to think about the issue of adequate access to food. The FAO defines food security as "a situation that exists when all people, at all times, have physical, social and economic access to sufficient, safe and nutritious *food* that meets their dietary needs and *food* preferences for an active and healthy life."[6] Food security usually refers to households, regions, or nations. In measuring food security, the FAO uses a suite of indicators with four dimensions: food availability, economic and physical access, stability over time, and utilization of food. Another useful measure of food security and hunger is the Global Hunger Index (GHI) reported by the International Food Policy Research Institute (IFPRI). The GHI takes into account three factors: the percent of a country's population suffering from undernourishment, the percent of children under the age of five who are underweight, and the mortality rate for children under the age of five. These various measures are useful in illustrating the extent of world hunger and food insecurity. And while world hunger and food insecurity are not the same thing, I use the terms interchangeably since each concept aims to measure, at a basic level, inadequate access to food.[7]

Despite global agreement at the World Food Summit and in the Millennium Development Goals to address world hunger and food insecurity, these issues remain significant problems faced by hundreds of millions of people around the world. A number of factors contribute to world hunger and food insecurity, but many discussions of hunger tend to focus on issues such as agricultural production and the supply of food. The perspective developed in this book, however, highlights the importance of accessibility to food, as well as the food supply. My aim here is not to provide a comprehensive explanation of hunger and food security. Rather, my goal in this chapter is to show how developments discussed in the previous chapter – in particular, divisions between food grains and feed grains, the end of the US food regime, and the shift toward liberalization in the world economy – have contributed to greater world hunger and reduced food security in specific ways.

Hunger and the Geopolitics of Grains in History

One fundamental link between grain markets and hunger lies in the grain trade. On the one hand, the grain trade can obviously help to alleviate hunger by providing needed imports for nations or populations that have low food supplies. On the other hand, the grain trade exists in the context of a capitalist world economy where grains and other commodities flow in the direction of profits rather than need. At various points in history, nations have actually exported grains during periods of food crisis or food insecurity.

Mike Davis examined the great famines in the late 1800s in countries such as India, China, and Brazil, which led to more than 30 million deaths. He showed how these deaths were, to a significant extent, the result of market dynamics that led to exports, even in times of hunger. Davis states that in British India, for example, there were "huge grain exports to England in the midst of horrendous starvation." Davis argues that the famines and hunger in the late 1800s were created by, to an important extent, the flow of exports, which was tied to incorporation of new regions into the world economy: "We . . . are dealing . . . with the fate of tropical humanity at the precise moment (1870–1914) when its labor and products were being dynamically conscripted into the London-centered world economy."[8] In the second half of the 1800s, regions within India developed into export districts focused on wheat or cotton production. The cotton and wheat from these regions, of course, were destined for Britain. Importantly, the establishment of wheat and cotton production displaced the subsistence agriculture that had occupied the area. Davis notes that in one such region of India "local food security was eroded not only by the advance of cotton production (which doubled in acreage in the last quarter of the century) but of grain exports as well. During the famine of 1899–1900, when 143,000 Beraris died directly from starvation, the province exported . . . an incredible 747,000 bushels of grain."[9] Consequently, areas of the world that had previously been food secure lost some portion of their access to food as they were incorporated into the world economy.

Figure 4.1 shows wheat exports from India during this time of famines and food insecurity. Indian wheat exports rose from just a few thousand metric tons to 280,000 MT in 1876 and 324,000 MT in 1877. While food insecurity and hunger were present throughout much of the period between

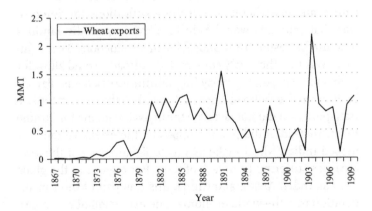

Figure 4.1. Wheat Exports from India, 1867–1910.

Source: Mitchell, B.R. (1998), *International Historical Statistics: Africa, Asia, and Oceania, 1750–1993,* New York: Macmillan, p. 340.

1870 and 1905, two periods of intense famine were 1876–9 and 1896–1902. This first period coincided with the initial explosion in Indian wheat exports. The second period, at the turn of the century, likewise saw wheat exports spike. And in between these two periods of famine, in the 1880s, Indian wheat exports reached over 1 MMT. Davis again highlights the connection between these rising exports and food insecurity in India: "In the main export districts . . . wheat occupied two-thirds of the acreage once devoted to subsistence grains."[10] The land that had produced grains for local consumption became land that produced wheat for export.

The broader context of the world economy of the late 1800s set the stage for such famines. Britain was the dominant world power in the late 1800s, and it constructed the rules of the world economy to support – or compel – free trade, including in agriculture. By the middle of the 1800s, Britain began to invest its surplus capital around the globe, particularly in the construction of railroads. Britain helped finance railroads in the US, continental Europe, Africa, India, Latin America, China, and elsewhere. One of the justifications for doing so was that railroads would help to alleviate periodic famines that might result from shortfalls in production. The argument was that the newly constructed railroads would allow for grains to be brought quickly into famine-struck areas. Britain built extensive railroad lines in India, but this new extensive transportation did not facilitate the arrival of grains for famine relief. Instead, it did just the opposite: the extensive railways helped Indian wheat make its way to Britain, even if the local area was suffering from lack of food. For regions of the globe such as India, Africa, and China, this was part of their incorporation into the world economy. The extraction of resources, including food and labor, went hand-in-hand with the expansion of railroads.

Most germane for our purposes, these regions became

important sources of grains for Britain and other European countries. As noted in Chapter 2, the British food regime rested on the principle of free trade. And throughout the second half of the nineteenth century, Britain imported more and more grain, particularly wheat. British wheat imports increased from 0.6 MMT in 1855 to 1.6 MMT in 1870 to 3.1 MMT in 1885. By 1905, Britain imported about 5 MMT of wheat per year. The growing Indian wheat exports helped to feed this expansion of British wheat imports.[11]

Karl Polanyi also recognized the significance of the market in creating these famines, and his analysis and arguments are worth revisiting here because they ultimately foreshadow many of the underlying dynamics of hunger and food security found today. Polanyi noted, "The actual source of famines in the last fifty years was the free marketing of grain combined with the local failure of incomes. . . . In former times small local stores had been held against harvest failure, but these had been discontinued or swept away into the big market."[12] That is, the grain reserves of the past were eliminated as these regions became incorporated into the world economy. The market and the political forces behind its expansion pushed for the elimination of the reserves for the sake of greater profits through their sale, often through exports.

We can see these dynamics at work in the series of famines that struck India in the 1870s and 1890s. In an ironic twist, India's agricultural production expanded significantly during this period. As Davis notes, "the cotton- and wheat-producing regions . . . were both dynamos of India's late-Victorian export economy and epicenters of mass mortality in the famines of the 1870s and 1890s."[13] That is, the famines struck hardest in the most productive agricultural regions in India. The fruits of agriculture were exported to Britain and elsewhere at low prices. This both reduced the supply of food in the regions and reduced incomes. At the very moment that India's agriculture expanded production to export to Britain, India was struck by famine. The supply of food that had been available for India in the past went to feed the mass of workers in Britain.

While these examples of grain markets exacerbating periods of hunger and famine may seem like the "ancient history" of the nineteenth century, we should consider what they suggest about our current era. Perhaps we should reflect on how changes in the world economy – such as the increased liberalization seen in Chapter 3 – might also facilitate hunger in particular nations or regions. In doing that, we are likely to see that there are indeed similar processes continuing today.

World Hunger and the Recent Geopolitics of Grains: The Food Crisis of 2008

In 2007 and 2008, world grain prices increased substantially, with prices for wheat and rice rising by more than 200 percent. Maize prices saw "similar though less dramatic price increases" at that time as well. This rise in prices made food less accessible for millions of people, and world hunger increased. For example, in Pakistan in 2008, 77 million suffered from hunger, representing almost half of that country's population and a 28 percent increase from March 2007 when 60 million people suffered from hunger. The FAO estimated that more than 840 million people worldwide were hungry each year between 2009 and 2011. And at one point, the FAO estimated that more than 1 billion people in the world were hungry in 2009, in the wake of the global food crisis.[14]

As food prices rose and the threat of hunger spread, more than 30 countries were struck by mass protests and riots. These protests contributed to political instability in dozens of countries. In January 2007, for example, protests erupted in Mexico in response to rising maize prices. Known in the press as the "Tortilla Riots," these protests involved tens of thousands of people and were in response to tortilla prices increasing by 70 percent nationally and as much as 400 percent in some parts of Mexico. The protests prompted the government to control prices and increase food security.[15] Many other countries experienced protests and riots in reaction to the rising food prices, such as in Haiti, where the prime minister was removed after a week of food riots in April 2008. Later in 2010, rising grain prices played a role in protests in Tunisia and Algeria, which then spread across the Middle East as the Arab Spring shook the region. High grain prices were fueling food riots and general protests across the globe, some of which contributed to policy shifts, violent confrontations, and even changes in political regimes. In this way, grains have the power to transform societies.[16]

While world hunger has steadily declined over the past 50 years, periodic global food crises – such as in 1972 and 2008 – have led to brief increases in the number of undernourished people.[17] Such food crises have not generally resulted from significant changes in the food supply or sharp increases in demand.[18] Instead, dynamics in world grain markets have contributed to food crises in fundamental ways. Several factors contributed to the spike in grain prices that drove the food crisis in 2008: restrictions imposed on rice exports, greater use of grains (especially maize) in biofuels, and the financialization of agriculture. Each of these factors demonstrates how the geopolitics of grains is essential to understanding such crises.

First, several countries imposed restrictions on rice exports in 2007 and 2008, and this was an important factor in the crisis in the global rice market. One might assume that these restrictions were put in place because of a shortage of rice. But as C. Peter Timmer and David Dawe point out, "The actual price panic that resulted, however, had little rationale in the fundamentals of supply and demand."[19] Between 2000 and

2008, world rice production increased by about 74 MMT, from 594 MMT to 668 MMT. Rather than being caused by low rice production or stocks (that is, rice carried over from previous years), the crisis in the world rice market can be seen as "due in large part to national" policy responses to a broader global context of uncertainty in grains, particularly wheat. That is, because of the instability in the world economy, rice became perceived as being in short supply. The policy responses of different nations reinforced that belief. India and Vietnam, each an important rice exporter, imposed restrictions on rice exports in 2007 and 2008, respectively. India, in fact, banned rice exports in an effort to reduce the amount of wheat it would need to import because wheat prices were already rising in 2007. Thailand, the world's leading rice exporter, did not impose restrictions on exports, but it nevertheless contributed to the market instability by announcing plans for restrictions as well as by proposing the creation of a rice exporter cartel, the Organization of Rice Exporting Countries. Even though only a small portion of rice produced worldwide is exported, these national policies limiting exports contributed to the spike in the price of rice. Countries imposed these restrictions in an attempt to stabilize both the domestic supply and the price of rice.

Second, in the years leading up to the global food crisis, several countries implemented national policies that expanded biofuels production. In the US, "the Bush administration set corn ethanol targets (35 billion gallons by 2017) with huge subsidies to the agribusiness giants ADM, Bunge, Cargill and others"[20] with the passage of the Energy Independence and Security Act of 2007. The next year, in the midst of the food crisis, about 30 percent of US maize went into biofuel production. This shift toward biofuel production in the US is especially important because it is the world's leading exporter of maize. Other countries, such as Brazil, also increased biofuel production, but they often used different agricultural commodities, such as sugar or oil palms. The EU also issued targets for increasing biofuels, much of which it gets through imports. The concern in cases like Brazil and the EU is that the expansion of biofuel production will reduce the land devoted to food production. This shift to biofuels, then, contributed to the global food crisis by (1) making world maize prices higher and less stable, and (2) encouraging some countries to shift away from food grains production.[21]

Third, in the decades leading up to the global food crisis, agriculture experienced greater financialization, which is increasingly treating food as a commodity and source of profits. While finance has played a role in agriculture and food for centuries, this has increased over the past few decades. One primary example of financialization can be seen in the commodity futures markets, which were created in Britain and the US in the 1800s to offer protection from market instability and price volatility. Basically, commodity futures are a way to set a price for a specified amount of wheat, for example, to be delivered on a particular date in the future. In the US, various regulations on futures trading were created in the 1920s and 1930s to limit price speculation and attempts to manipulate prices, and the Commodities Futures Trading Commission (CFTC) enforced these regulations. Over the past 30 years or so, however, these regulations have weakened. In the 1980s, banks became permitted to sell commodity investment funds (CIFs) outside of the futures markets, and the CFTC removed some of the regulations and oversight on banks' trading activities in CIFs in 1991. In 2000, the Commodity Futures Modernization Act exempted CIFs from CFTC oversight, thereby allowing for more speculation in futures trading. After the collapse of the real estate and housing markets by about 2007, financial investors sought other tangible commodities in which to invest. Many investors turned toward food, especially grains. Consequently, a substantial amount of capital flowed into commodities markets, buying up different kinds of grains and other foods. Investments in CIFs increased from US$15 billion in 2003 to US$200 billion in 2008, and CIF "investment in soy, corn, wheat, cattle, and hogs ballooned to US$47 billion in 2007, up from US$10 billion just a year earlier."[22] Because commodities markets actually sell quantities of grains, this influx of investment capital drove up world grain prices. As already noted, this was a more important factor for maize and wheat markets than for the global rice market, in part because futures markets for rice are "thinly traded, and there is little opportunity for financial speculation in rice prices."[23] Nevertheless, the instability in wheat and maize prices caused by this influx of capital played a role in the creation of restrictions on rice exports in countries like India and Vietnam.

How do these factors – rice export restrictions, expansion in biofuels, and financialization of agriculture – relate to the geopolitics of grains discussed in previous chapters? These three factors are best understood as immediate or proximate factors that contributed to the global food crisis within a particular world economic context. This context, however, was neither natural nor mere coincidence. Rather, the very trends discussed in Chapter 3 laid the foundation for this context. The liberalization of agriculture in the world economy beginning in the 1970s created greater instability in market prices as the national and international policies that helped to stabilize grain production, prices, and trade during the US food regime were weakened. The increased financialization of agriculture, especially regarding futures markets, was part of a broader effort to reduce or eliminate restrictions on finance capital. The large shift of US grains into biofuels was facilitated by the elimination of production controls, which required farmers to stick with a particular commodity to remain eligible for subsidies. Thus, these secular processes – the expansion of liberalization and the end of supply management – laid the foundation for the world economic context in which the global food crisis occurred in 2008.

Food Security and the Geopolitics of Grains

Just as food crises are linked to grain markets, so too is the more general issue of food security. While food crises are periodic disruptions in access to food in the world economy, the concept of food security is about the ongoing and continual access to food, or lack thereof. A variety of factors – including wars, natural disasters, and extreme weather – may reduce food security by decreasing a population's access to food or by reducing the supply of food. Food security and world hunger, however, are more complex than simply increasing the aggregate food supply. For example, Craig Jenkins and Steven Scanlan point out that "Despite the 'green revolution' and the significant growth in international food aid and assistance, between 1970 and 1990 almost half of the world's less developed countries (LDCs) suffered a decline in aggregate food supply, and more than a quarter suffered from an increase in child hunger."[24] Even with increased use of agricultural technologies, increased agricultural production in the world, and increased food aid, the supply of food in many countries still declined. Thus, we need to ask what other factors lay behind the availability, accessibility, and even the supply of food. In particular, we need to examine grain markets and the geopolitics of grains.

Agricultural Exports and Food Security
Food security is frequently seen as an issue of food production and food imports. The export of grains, for example, is generally not seen as a detriment to food security. Rather, the

export of grains or other food is seen as having a couple of important benefits. First, such exports help to facilitate the development of agriculture by drawing resources in the form of investments, since export agriculture generates revenues. Second, agricultural exports increase national income and allow for greater food imports. In this perspective, Brazil is often held up as a model of development. Brazil has substantially increased its agricultural production and exports at the same time that food insecurity has decreased within the country. This perspective on food exports, however, has significant problems. In the case of Brazil, for example, food security was improved through the Fome Zero (Zero Hunger) policy initiated by President Luiz Ignácio Lula da Silva in 2003, during a period when Brazil's GDP per capita increased by 3.5 percent per year (2003–8) and there were significant improvements in incomes for the poorest people in Brazil. Therefore, specific poverty-reducing policies were put into place to help facilitate the redistribution of income and reduce poverty in Brazil.[25]

Furthermore, we have already seen instances in history in which nations have exported wheat and rice, even while their own populations suffered from hunger. Yet, we can also find several instances of such patterns today, as well. Although many grain-exporting nations (particularly, rice-exporting) put restrictions on exports in 2008 and thereby exacerbated world price increases, in other instances nations have actually exported grains during periods of food crisis or food insecurity. Therefore, food exports can contribute to hunger in important ways, as research has found that "export-oriented production causes food cultivation and access to be geared away from meeting local consumption needs."[26]

We see similar dynamics still at work today in South Asia, a region that is among the most food insecure in the world, with a GHI rating similar to that of much of Sub-Saharan Africa. For example, India and Pakistan are two of the most food

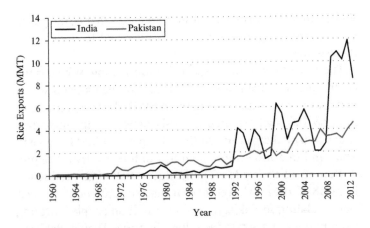

Figure 4.2. Rice Exports from India and Pakistan, 1960–2015.

Source: Foreign Agricultural Service, USDA, "PS&D Online Database."

insecure nations in the world with GHI ratings of "serious."[27] These two countries have experienced significant food insecurity for the past 20 years, as well as "alarming" levels of food insecurity as recently as 2011. Yet as Figure 4.2 shows, India and Pakistan have each exported substantial quantities of rice during the past 20 years. And while these two countries were experiencing "alarming" levels of food insecurity, they also exported increasing amounts of rice during the 2008 food crisis. In fact, Pakistan also exported substantial amounts of wheat, as well. Figure 4.2 shows that India's rice exports decreased significantly in 2008 and 2009, but Pakistan's rice exports continued during this food crisis and even reached a peak in 2009. Furthermore, India's rice exports increased substantially in 2010, even though it had a GHI rating of "alarming" at that time. Again, the role of export-oriented agriculture is fundamentally important to understanding issues of food security and hunger. Therefore, food insecurity and hunger are not primarily about the production of food.

Rather, market processes and state policies – that is, the political economy of grains – must be considered to understand these issues.

The case of Pakistan is especially illuminating. Wheat is the central grain in Pakistan, and the country had a good wheat harvest in 2008 with more than 20 MMT. In 2007 and again in 2008, Pakistan exported 2.1 MMT of wheat – the most ever exported by Pakistan. In addition, it exported 3 MMT of rice in 2007 and in 2008 – more than half of the country's rice production in 2007 (5.7 MMT) and almost half of its production in 2008 (6.9 MMT). Yet, at that historical moment, hunger was escalating in Pakistan, from 60 million people suffering from hunger in 2007 to 77 million in 2008. That is, Pakistan exported about 5 MMT of wheat and rice combined in each of these years, while at the same time hunger increased by 28 percent. Why did Pakistan, a country that for almost 20 years had its food security situation labeled "serious" according to the GHI, decide to increase its wheat and rice exports significantly at the very moment that a global food crisis was emerging?

The short answer, of course, centers on grain prices. Certainly for rice, Pakistan had been an exporting nation for several years – again, despite having a high GHI rating. Pakistan was one of the few rice-exporting nations not to restrict exports in 2008. In fact, in 2008 the government instituted minimum export prices to encourage exports. More interesting, though, is the explanation for increased wheat exports, especially since wheat is the primary grain in Pakistan. Saadia Toor notes that the food crisis in Pakistan "manifested itself as a wheat shortage in 2008 . . . [but] the problem was not a shortfall in wheat production."[28] Toor highlights a couple of factors that contributed to the crisis in Pakistan. First, the IMF and World Bank encouraged Pakistan to sell its wheat reserves to take advantage of rising world prices in 2007. Second, the government in Pakistan reduced subsidies to wheat farmers, thereby encouraging a shift to other crops such as sugar cane or rice. Together, these factors pushed wheat prices in Pakistan higher by reducing the over-all supply. Most importantly for our purposes, the high world prices for wheat and the IMF and World Bank all encouraged Pakistan to sell its wheat reserves through the export market, even though prices were rising, food insecurity remained high, and hunger was spreading within that nation.

Again, this is not to say that grain markets or exports cause hunger. The point is to understand the role of grain markets and the political economy of exports, especially during times of hunger and food crisis. There are important examples of nations exporting food – as Pakistan did in 2008 – despite rising hunger within their population. The frequent empha-sis on agricultural production as a solution to hunger, then, is misplaced, at least in some cases. The issues of world hunger and food security are far more complex than the amount of food produced. Just because a country increases its agricul-tural production does not necessarily mean that hunger will decrease and food security will increase. That increase in food production may well be sent to where profits are high-est, thereby leaving perhaps even more people suffering from hunger. Yet, grain markets can affect hunger and food secu-rity in more ways than just facilitating exports. Grain markets can also affect what farmers produce.

Food Security and Markets: The Case of Quinoa
We can find another example of how markets can affect food security in the case of quinoa, which is grown primar-ily in the Andes region of South America. Quinoa is a grain crop grown for its edible seeds, but it is a chenopod, which means that it is closely related to spinach and beetroots. Its seeds can be ground into flour, toasted, or consumed like rice

or cous cous. Quinoa can be stored for about a decade when it is dried. Because it is high in protein and contains significant amounts of iron, fiber, calcium, and vitamins, quinoa has come to be seen as a "superfood" in developed countries like Canada, Japan, and the US, as well as Europe and elsewhere. Furthermore, quinoa is a resilient crop in terms of drought, salinized soil, and extreme temperatures. It is worth considering the case of quinoa in our discussion of food security, in part because quinoa is frequently cited as a possible solution to the issues of food security and world hunger, given its nutrition density and climate resiliency.

Quinoa production originated in the Andes in South America, and it has been an important part of the diet in that region for at least 3,000 years. With the Spanish conquest of South America, quinoa receded as a part of indigenous diets because the Spanish forbade its production. The Spanish accepted potatoes, which also originated in the Andes, as a food crop rather than quinoa. This grain regained some of its prominence when South Americans won independence from the Spanish in the early 1800s, but it was not until the 1990s that global quinoa consumption really took off.

With the recent increase in the global consumption of quinoa, two concerns have arisen regarding the implications of this trend. First, some observers have expressed concern that increased global demand for quinoa will threaten the food security of small farmers in South America – particularly, Bolivia, Ecuador, and Peru – by leading to changes in production or landownership. Second, others worry that the increased global demand for quinoa will drive up prices in these South American countries where quinoa is a central component of traditional diets.

As Figure 4.3 shows, global quinoa production has increased dramatically, especially during the past few decades. In 1968, global quinoa production was only 15,000 MT, but

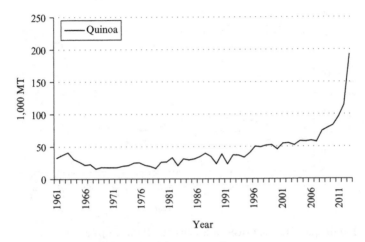

Figure 4.3. World Quinoa Production, 1961–2014.

Source: Food and Agriculture Organization, United Nations, "FAOSTAT."

it was 103,000 MT in 2013. Much of this increase in global production has occurred during the past 20 years: global quinoa production increased from about 23,000 MT in 1992 to almost 58,000 MT in 2008, but an even sharper increase has been seen more recently, as global production nearly doubled from 2008 to 2013. Then, quinoa production increased even more sharply in 2014, rising to 192,000 MT. With this increased production, international trade has also increased in quinoa. Bolivia and Peru are the world's largest quinoa producers, and the primary consumers of quinoa are the US, Canada, and Germany. Thus, richer countries in the world economy are now important consumers of this food produced in poorer countries.

The increased production and trade of quinoa has important benefits and potential problems where hunger is concerned. On the one hand, the increased demand for quinoa presents an important source of potential income for poor Andean

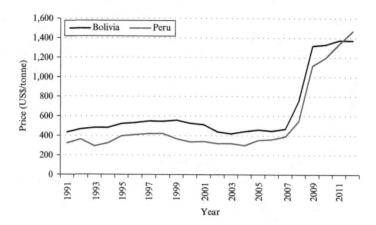

Figure 4.4. Quinoa Prices in Bolivia and Peru, 1991–2012.
Source: Food and Agriculture Organization, United Nations, "FAOSTAT."

farmers in Bolivia, Ecuador, and Peru. The FAO even designated 2013 as the International Year of Quinoa. On the other hand, increased international demand for quinoa has the potential to cause large outflows of this grain, which is a central component of diets for the people in these regions of South America. It also has the potential to contribute to increased prices for quinoa, which may increase the risk of local populations not being able to afford this important grain. Figure 4.4 shows the rise in quinoa prices in Bolivia and Peru. While the higher prices might mean higher income, they also mean that quinoa is less accessible for domestic consumption.[29]

Grains, Meat Production, and World Hunger
In Chapter 3, we saw that meat production and consumption increased substantially in the twentieth century. Between 1975 and 2000, the world's population increased by about 50 percent, and per capita meat consumption increased by about 35 percent. And in 2011, about 6.9 billion people con-

sumed an average of 39 kg of meat per capita. On the one hand, increased meat consumption can be seen as a sign of increasing incomes and, therefore, a lower likelihood of hunger. And this is true to some extent. Meat consumption tends to rise as incomes rise and middle classes grow in size. So increased meat consumption is, in some respects, an indicator of rising incomes, falling poverty, and decreasing world hunger.

However, the processes involved in expanding meat production and consumption create a situation in which some populations may be more vulnerable to food crises, and most importantly these processes also indicate a redistribution of resources important to agriculture and the world food supply: land, grains, and water. Briefly put, meat production requires far more resources – more land, more grains, and more water – to produce calories for human consumption than does the production of more plants, including grains. Countries that are food insecure and increase meat production, then, allocate important resources in ways that are not aimed at alleviating hunger. Another way to think about this is to ask, for whom are grains being produced? Who will consume the expansion in grains?

We can see this in India, a country described as having a "serious" food insecurity problem, with 17 percent of its population suffering from undernourishment between 2011 and 2013. Figure 4.5 shows that beef production has increased significantly and steadily since 1996. In fact, following the 2008 food crisis, beef production in India has increased from 2.5 MMT in 2009 to 4.1 MMT in 2015. More importantly, beef exports have risen sharply since the food crisis of 2008. India's beef exports increased from 0.6 MMT in 2009 to 2 MMT in 2014, when India exported almost half of the beef it produced. This made India the largest beef exporter in the world in 2014, accounting for 20 percent of all beef exports and surpassing Brazil, Australia, and the US. Indian beef

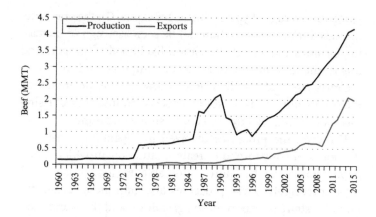

Figure 4.5. Indian Beef Production and Exports, 1960–2015.

Source: Foreign Agricultural Service, USDA, "PS&D Online Database."

exports go to Southeast Asia (e.g., Vietnam, Thailand, and Malaysia), Australia, and the Middle East (e.g., Saudi Arabia, UAE, and Egypt). Following the food crisis in 2008, beef production and beef exports grew almost the same amount, 1.6 MMT and 1.4 MMT, respectively. This beef production, then, is not aimed at alleviating hunger in India. The resources used in meat production – particularly, land, water, and grains – are put to use not in reducing food insecurity in the country but for commercial exports.[30]

On the one hand, beef production in India might be viewed as relatively environmentally friendly. Most cows, buffalo, and other animals live most of their lives in pasture and not in confined animal feeding operations (CAFOs). For cows, in particular, this is because the dairy industry in India is among the largest in the world: India had 123 million dairy cows in 2014, which is about half the world's total and about 85 million more than Brazil, the country with the second most dairy cows. And, much of India's diary production is based on small farms. Because of widespread dairy production in India and the size of the dairy industry, India has the largest number of cattle in the world at about 300 million, more than triple the number of cows in the US – despite the fact that India's population is about 80 percent and holds cows as sacred, and the government has banned killing cows for meat or exporting beef.

On the other hand, beef production uses a large amount of water, regardless of the treatment of cows – or buffalo. In fact, around the world – even in the US – cows raised for slaughter spend only the last portion of their lives in CAFO settings, going from pastures to feed lots in the last few months of their lives for fattening before slaughter. Nonetheless, according to the UK's Institution of Mechanical Engineers, to produce 1 kg of beef requires 15,400 liters of water, which is far more water than required to produce most grains, legumes, vegetables, or fruits. Thus, the sharp increase in beef production also suggests a sharp increase in water usage.[31]

For India, this is a particularly important point because India faces a potential water crisis. The World Bank has recently warned that water supplies in India are threatened by climate change, the growing population, and inefficiencies related to the country's underdeveloped infrastructure. One part of this potential crisis is centered on clean drinking water, but another concern is that the availability of replenishable water resources may become increasingly threatened. The expansion of agriculture, including grain production and especially meat production, also is likely to put further stress on India's aquifers.

Finally, the primary point here is that India is the world's largest beef exporter at a time when it is still one of the most food insecure countries in the world. Land that might be used to produce grains, legumes, or other food crops has increasingly been used in the production of feed grains, in particular maize and soybeans. As Figure 4.6 shows, the amount of

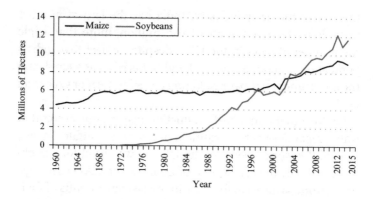

Figure 4.6. Maize and Soybean Production in India, 1960–2015.
Source: Foreign Agricultural Service, USDA, "PS&D Online Database."

land devoted to soybean production doubled between 2000 and 2015, from 5.8 million hectares to 11.7 million hectares. The amount of land used for maize production also increased during this period, though the rise was less dramatic: from 6.5 million hectares in 2002 to 9 million hectares in 2015. While this expansion in land used for feed grains helped with the increase in beef production, maize exports have also increased since 2002, reaching a peak of almost 4.7 MMT in 2012. Again, keep in mind that this expansion in the production and export of feed grains and beef occurred in a country that had a food security situation categorized as "serious" (17.9) on the GHI in 2014.

India's beef exports beg comparison to the grain exports in the late 1800s. Of course, India is not experiencing the famines seen over a hundred years ago. Nonetheless, the level of food insecurity in the country necessarily draws focus on the role of the market in shaping agricultural production and trade in ways that do not lead to greater access to food for the population – just as occurred at the turn of the previous century. Perhaps most notably, while India was a British colony being drawn into the world economy – and world grain markets – during the great famines, India is today an independent democracy. No other country is compelling particular production patterns in agriculture in India now, but the market certainly is playing a role.

Other countries are in situations not unlike India's, though most export far less meat, if any. On a global scale, then, the economic competition between food grains and feed grains continues. As feed grain and meat production expands, choices must be made regarding the allocation of important resources, such as land and water. When a priority is placed on high-value production (i.e., profitability) rather than access for the overall population, then less inefficient food production through feed grains and meat production is likely preferred, increasingly through industrial methods (e.g., CAFOs). This competition between food grains and feed grains will continue to shape access to food in a number of countries for years to come.

The Geopolitics of Grains and Addressing World Hunger

As Ray Bush notes, "The global food 'crisis' is as much about poor people being unable to sustain their *access* to food, and is thus about poverty, power and politics, as it is about issues of production, productivity and contested debate about technological quick fixes to population growth."[32] This has been true for food crises and world hunger, more generally, dating back at least to the middle 1800s. The market has regularly played a central role in food crises, world hunger, and food insecurity. The production and movement of grains in the market is strongly influenced by profitability.

The division between food grains and feed grains also links

to the issues of hunger, food insecurity, and food crises. For example, as this chapter has discussed, there is the role that feed grain production and meat consumption play in world hunger, as meat production uses significant grain, water, and land resources. Not only does the expansion of feed grains and meat production have the potential to divert grain production or distribution away from food to more expensive meat, but increased meat production also has the potential to use important resources (e.g., water and land). In addition, small farmers may be displaced in this process.

The argument that technology can alleviate hunger and improve food security by increasing production stands in the face of the trends presented in this chapter. Furthermore, understanding patterns of technology adoption, such as for genetic engineering, requires us to consider divisions between grains, particularly the now-familiar division between food grains and feed grains. That is where we turn our attention in the next chapter.

CHAPTER FIVE

Genetically Engineered Grains

In the 1990s, Aventis Crop Science developed StarLink maize, a genetically engineered (GE) variety of maize that contained a *Bacillus thuringiensis* (Bt) gene called Cry9C to make it resistant to insects – in particular, a caterpillar called the European corn borer. This Bt gene is a toxin that kills the larvae of the European corn borer. Cry9C is also heat resistant, making it difficult for the human gastrointestinal tract to break it down, which means that StarLink might produce allergies in humans. Consequently, the US Environmental Protection Agency (USEPA) approved StarLink for animal consumption but not for direct human consumption. This approval came in 1998, and production of StarLink for animal feed expanded substantially over the next two years.[1]

In 2000, Genetically Engineered Food Alert (GEFA), an advocacy group opposed to genetic engineering in agriculture, began testing food products for evidence of GE crops. In September of that year, GEFA announced that an independent lab had found StarLink maize in Kraft Food's "Taco Bell Home Originals" brand taco shells. Kraft Foods had bought maize for its food products from a mill in Texas that used maize from six states and, at the time, did not segregate GE corn and conventionally grown corn. Kraft recalled the products and suspended production of them. Other food companies and retailers did the same: Safeway supermarkets recalled its store brand of taco shells, Mission Foods recalled over 300 products, a Kellogg's plant stopped production, and

ConAgra Foods recalled a dozen of its cornmeal products – all because of evidence that StarLink maize was used or concern that it might have been used in production. Even some soup mixes were recalled, and Tyson Foods announced that it would not use StarLink maize in its chicken production process. StarLink maize had made its way into the US food system.

This crisis resulted in Aventis creating a program to buy back StarLink maize and redirect it into animal or ethanol production. The US Department of Agriculture (USDA) also agreed to spend up to US$20 million as part of this buy back effort. In addition, several lawsuits were brought by Taco Bell franchisees, large minority owners of Taco Bell, a few consumers claiming to have suffered allergic reactions to StarLink maize, and farmers who did not plant StarLink maize. Aventis withdrew the registration for StarLink, and the company was bought by Bayer in 2001.[2]

The reach of the crisis went beyond US borders. StarLink was found in tortillas in South Korea, and it was also found in snack foods and animal feed in Japan. Korea announced plans to find alternate sources for its maize imports, turning from the US to Latin America. StarLink maize was also found in US food aid sent to Latin American countries. US maize exports to some countries were disrupted, though overall exports showed little effect as the US continued to account for about 50 percent of the world's maize exports. By 2002, however, US maize exports dropped by about 20 percent, from 48 MMT in 2001 to 40 MMT. Perhaps even more notably, maize exports from Brazil increased from just 0.2 MMT in 1999 to more than 6 MMT in 2000. Brazil's maize exports climbed steadily after 2000, reaching more than 20 percent of total world maize exports by 2010. As we will see, however, Brazil also adopted GE maize and soybean production, following the lead of the US.

The crisis around StarLink's entrance into the food system reflects several fundamental issues discussed in the preceding chapters and how they relate to biotechnology in agriculture. First, StarLink was allowed into the food system as a feed grain, but this GE crop became disruptive when it was used as a food grain for direct consumption. As we will see, farmers, consumers, and even some food companies have been more resistant to GE food grains, but GE feed grains have been more readily accepted in some countries. Second, GE crops have implications for international trade in agriculture. With the advent of GE maize and soybeans, the dominance of the US in world grain markets declined. Finally, biotechnology simply has potential implications for how people eat – and implicitly, then, it has potential implications for world hunger. Some people have argued that GE crops have the potential to significantly curb, if not end, world hunger. Yet, issues of corporate control, market processes, and national policies all influence the likelihood of this.

This chapter explores this range of issues: the division between food grains and feed grains, as it appears in biotechnology; GE crops in the world economy and international trade; resistance to (or acceptance of) GE crops by farmers, consumers, corporations, and other groups; and how corporate control is connected with biotechnology. Before focusing on these issues, however, it is important first to have a clear understanding of biotechnology and genetic engineering.

What are Genetically Engineered Seeds and Foods?

Genetic engineering began in the 1970s, and involves the manipulation of an organism's DNA – "the genetic information within every cell that allows living things to function, grow, and reproduce." In this process, the genes of one organism are transferred to another organism, giving the latter some trait or traits found in the former. As social scientist Abby Kinchy puts it, "Genetic engineering allows plant breeders to create plants with characteristics that would have been difficult or impossible to develop through traditional breeding."[3] GE crops have some specialized trait that would be difficult or even impossible to create through traditional plant breeding techniques.

Researchers have identified three generations of GE crops, with each generation having new traits with different functions. The first generation of GE crops involves the use of genetic traits that enhance some aspect of the growing of the crop – in particular, herbicide tolerance, insect resistance, or resistance to environmental stress, such as drought. First generation GE traits relate to the level of the farmer and production. The second generation of GE crops centers on enhancements at the level of the consumer, using genetic traits that enhance nutrition or flavor (including greater nutritional value for animal feed). And the third generation of GE crops "would include traits to allow production of pharmaceuticals and products beyond traditional food and fiber."[4] By far, most GE crops grown commercially today are first generation, with GE traits that relate to the production process at the level of the farm. Furthermore, most – but by no means all – of these commercially available first generation GE crops are grains.

The first GE food to reach consumers in the US was neither first generation nor a grain. It was the "Flavr Savr" tomato, developed in 1982 and commercially released in 1994. Calgene – a company since bought by Monsanto – produced this tomato, which was genetically engineered to delay ripening and make these tomatoes last longer and remain firmer in stores and transport. While the Flavr Savr tomato saw some success in sales in the US, high production and distribution costs prevented this GE food from being profitable.

Consequently, it was pulled from production in the US largely due to economic considerations rather than consumer resistance, though this was an issue in Europe.[5]

In contrast to the Flavr Savr tomato, which was a second generation GE crop, most GE crops commercially available today, as noted above, are first generation with traits focused on production, primarily herbicide tolerance or insect resistance. Several GE crops – including maize, soybeans, canola, alfalfa, sugar beets, papaya, and squash – have added traits that allow herbicide tolerance (HT). HT crops can be used with certain herbicides, particularly glyphosate-based herbicides such as Monsanto's Roundup. GE crops that are insect resistant contain *Bacillus thuringiensis* (Bt), a gene from the soil bacterium that produces a protein that is toxic to certain insects. Maize is the only grain that has a Bt variety that is commercially available, and maize is frequently stacked – meaning that it is both HT and Bt. Most of the production of GE crops, both in the US and globally, are HT or Bt crops. Therefore, GE traits overwhelmingly tend to be focused on just two production issues: reducing damage from insects, and increasing tolerance to and for use with a particular herbicide. The vast range of potential GE crops with second and third generation traits has yet to be realized commercially.

Similarly, just a few crops dominate GE production: maize, soybeans, cotton, and canola. These four crops account for almost all GE production globally. Soybeans and maize, by far, account for most of the GE grain production in the US and globally. In 2003, maize, soybeans, and canola accounted for more than 85 percent of all hectares planted with GE crops in the US. Globally, soybeans, maize, and cotton accounted for 95 percent of hectares devoted to GE crop production in 2010. As already indicated, GE soybeans, maize, canola, and cotton have either HT or Bt traits, or both. So this small range of crops that account for almost all of the world's GE production have either one or both of just two GE traits. There is little diversity among GE crops.[6]

One addition and important point about these GE crops is that they are feed grains (aside from cotton, of course). While maize is both a feed grain and food grain, its status as a leading feed grain leads it to be one of the primary GE crops. The oils from these seeds – corn oil, soybean oil, canola oil, and cottonseed oil – are all used regularly in processed foods. Consequently, GE crops make there way directly into the food system as oils in cookies, breads, ready made dinners, condiments, sauces, and so on. GE maize appears as a grain in many processed foods, most obviously corn chips. Yet, neither GE rice nor GE wheat is currently commercially available. While companies have conducted research and developed GE wheat and rice, these GE crops have not entered the food system. Most GE crop production is in feed grains.

GE grains are most widespread in the US food system, particularly for maize and soybeans. Since 1996, when GE maize and soybeans first became commercially available, the number of hectares in the US planted with GE crops increased from about 7 percent for soybeans and about 3 percent for maize to 94 percent for soybeans and 92 percent for maize in 2015. As Figure 5.1 shows, the adoption of GE maize and soybeans expanded rather quickly in the US, especially for soybeans. Despite the crisis surrounding StarLink maize in the food system, then, US farmers continued to expand their adoption and production of genetically engineered crops, particularly soybeans and even maize. In 2013, more than 87 million acres of GE maize and 72 million acres of GE soybeans were planted in the US.[7]

Globally, the adoption of GE crops has likewise spread. In 1996, the global area devoted to GE crops covered about 1.7 million hectares. In 2014, GE crops covered about 181 million hectares globally. Despite this seemingly wide reach, only

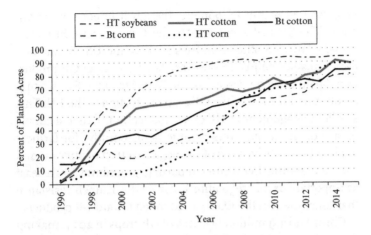

Figure 5.1. Adoption of Genetically Engineered Crops in the United States, 1996–2015.

Source: Economic Research Service, USDA, available at http://www.ers.usda.gov/media/185551/biotechcrops_d.html.

28 countries grew GE crops in 2014; in other words, about 14 percent of the countries in the world grew GE crops that year. Even more notably, however, GE production is concentrated in just a few countries: the US, Brazil, Argentina, India, and Canada. In 2014, the US was the global leader, having planted 73 million hectares, accounting for 40 percent of the world's total GE hectares. Brazil was second with 42 million hectares, Argentina had 24 million hectares, and Canada and India each planted 11 hectares. Together, these five countries accounted for almost 90 percent of all GE hectares. (The US and Brazil accounted for more than 60 percent of the total global GE hectares.) Thus, global GE crop production is clearly concentrated in just a few countries, led by the US.[8]

In the EU, five countries were engaged in GE crop production in 2014: the Czech Republic, Portugal, Romania, Slovakia, and Spain. The EU allows only one GE crop – Bt maize – to be cultivated within its borders, though it imports more GE crops. The EU had about 143,000 hectares growing Bt maize. Thus, relative to other countries such as the US, Brazil, and even Canada, the EU devotes very few hectares to GE production. Spain grew 92 percent of the Bt maize in the EU in 2014, accounting for most of the GE crop production in the EU. This smaller engagement in GE crop production is due to a couple of factors. Some observers point to "a disincentive for farmers to plant Bt maize because of the negative effect of onerous and over-demanding EU farmer reporting procedures."[9] At least as important as any regulations may be the staunch resistance that consumers in the EU have exhibited toward GE products.

China had 3.9 million hectares of GE crops in 2014, making it sixth in the world for GE production. China's GE production did not focus on grains, but instead included cotton, papaya, poplar, tomatoes, and sweet peppers. Almost all of China's GE crop production is in cotton: China planted 3.9 million hectares of Bt cotton in 2014; the remaining GE crops were each planted on fewer than 10,000 hectares. Though its agricultural production does not currently include them, GE grains are nonetheless a central component of China's food system. In 2015, China imported 80 MMT of soybeans and 3 MMT of maize. These imports were likely to have been GE soybeans and maize, given the primary exporters of each commodity are the US and Brazil. Some observers have suggested that China may be a market for GE corn, soybeans, and even rice as the country grapples with expanding its own agricultural production and meeting the needs of its large population. Certainly, China is willing to accept GE soybeans and maize as imports, and it currently supports research into genetic engineering in agriculture. But there are still signs of hesitancy, as seen in a statement by President Xi JinPing that Chinese concerns and doubts about GE crops are understandable because of the relative newness of the technology. Nevertheless, the Chinese

Ministry of Agriculture has conducted a public campaign to highlight the potential benefits of GE crops to the Chinese.[10]

Finally, just a handful of global seed companies dominate the market for GE seeds. Monsanto, DuPont, and Syngenta are currently the largest seed companies in the world, and they each have extensive influence in the GE seed market. These three companies accounted for about 61 percent of the global seed market in 2009: Monsanto had about 27 percent, DuPont about 17 percent, and Syngenta had about 9 percent. Between 1996 and 2013, the seed industry became much more concentrated as hundreds of mergers, acquisitions, and alliances occurred. Monsanto, DuPont, and Syngenta were among the leaders in this drive toward a more concentrated market, but other companies followed suit, including BASF, Bayer, Dow, Limagrain, and Land-O-Lakes.[11]

Prior to the 1990s, the seed industry was largely a competitive market with a substantial number of firms. The advent of genetic engineering in agriculture facilitated increased concentration in the seed industry because it gave greater control over seeds to companies. For example, Monsanto is the largest global seed company today, but it was not involved in the seed industry before the mid-1980s. Since 1996, Monsanto has been the most active of the global seed companies in market consolidation, engaging in at least 31 acquisitions or mergers to gain ownership of other seed or pharmaceutical companies and spending several billion dollars in the process.[12]

This wave of mergers and consolidation in the agricultural biotech industry served two purposes. First, it was a way to separate biotechnology in medicine from biotechnology in agriculture. Biotechnology in medicine had much more widespread public acceptance in the form of vaccines and drugs. In the US, for example, there are more than 100 drugs and vaccines that are produced through genetic engineering. By contrast, biotechnology in agriculture was facing more public resistance and greater regulatory oversight, and even bans on production in some countries when this wave of consolidation and mergers occurred in the 1990s and early 2000s. Therefore, pharmaceutical and chemical companies, like DuPont and Monsanto, aimed to separate out biotechnology in medicine from that in agriculture.

Second, this wave of consolidation in biotech agriculture reflected efforts to achieve a greater degree of vertical integration within the global seed industry. DuPont and Monsanto had been primarily chemical companies, but each acquired seed companies in the 1990s. DuPont acquired Pioneer Hi-Breed in 1997, which was the world's largest seed company. Beginning in 1996, Monsanto acquired a number of seed companies including Dekalb Genetics, which was the second largest seed company in the US; Sementes Agroceres, a Brazilian maize seed company; Asgrow Agronomics, the largest soybean dealer in the US; and the International Division of Cargill, the world's largest seed dealer. With this burst of consolidation in the global seed market Monsanto, DuPont, and other companies aimed to merge their biotechnology capacity with the distribution power of the seed companies they acquired.[13]

Agricultural biotechnology, including genetic engineering, has been swallowed up by the current of the market economy, the drive for profit. Genetic engineering, in particular, has provided a technology that more easily allows the capture of profits by companies. Consequently, concentration in the seed industry increased substantially with the introduction and expansion of commercially available GE seeds. Nonetheless, others have pointed out that companies have had a difficult time achieving adequate returns on investment. The most commercially successful GE crops have been those which provide economic benefits at the point of production, such as greater crop yields due to reductions in the amount of crops lost to insects. And, GE crops that are linked to other products, specifically herbicides, have been profitable because they have also increased the usage of particular herbicides. The best example of this, of course, is Monsanto's Roundup herbicide and Roundup Ready GE seeds. Roundup is now the most-used herbicide in the world. Other GE crops that have created changes at the point of consumption – for example, increased nutrition or altered flavors – have not seen commercial success or been as profitable as first generation GE crops. Consequently, GE production follows the profitability.[14]

In sum, the story of GE crops is one of concentration and little variation: just a few traits dominate GE crops, only a few crops have GE varieties that are commercially available and widely used, only a handful of countries produce the vast majority of GE crops, and just a few global companies dominate the production of GE seeds. Yet, the strength and even the presence of resistance to GE crops vary across different countries as well as by commodity type. How can we explain the acceptance of and resistance to GE grains? Most explanations tend to focus on the logic of arguments (e.g., the "rationality" of acceptance and science, the "emotion" of resistance) or the power of corporations, specifically seed companies. In answering this question, this chapter focuses on farmers, consumers, and companies. I also examine how the roles of these actors in GE grains differ, if at all, between food grains and feed grains. Let us first take a look at the acceptance of GE grains, and then we will move on to resistance.

Adoption and Acceptance of Genetically Engineered Grains

Geographically, GE grains have been most accepted in the US, where the adoption rate of GE for some crops has surpassed

90 percent of farmers. In the US, GE seeds account for about 90 percent of the planted acres of maize and soybeans, as well as cotton. A few other countries also have high adoption rates for some GE grains, most notably canola in Canada (95 percent), and soybeans and maize in Brazil (92 percent and 75 percent, respectively) and Argentina (100 percent and 85 percent, respectively). The adoption of GE crops has been much slower in the EU, as we saw earlier, where various regulations severely limit the planting of GE crops.[15] Why have GE crops been so readily accepted in the US? How have some GE crops spread so rapidly in the global food system?

We might start to answer these questions by simply looking at the benefits of GE crops for farmers, agrifood corporations, and consumers. For farmers, GE crops can have some notable benefits, especially regarding first generation GE crops that focus on production. Chief among these is improved resistance to pests. Bt maize, for example, makes maize resistant to insects, and this increases the average yield. By increasing yield and therefore overall production by reducing crop loss to pests, Bt maize increases farmers' incomes. At the same time, Bt maize reduces farmers' expenditures by decreasing the need to purchase pesticide applications. Similarly, GE crops that are HT allow farmers to use herbicides deemed to be more effective, particularly glyphosates. While HT maize or soybeans may not reduce farmers' need for herbicide as an input, these GE crops do allow the adoption of herbicides that would otherwise not be an option. And studies have shown that Bt and HT GE crops tend to reduce pesticide use, increase yield, and raise farm income.[16]

This kind of acceptance can even be found among US food grain farmers. In their research on wheat farmers in the state of Washington, Raymond Jussuame and his colleagues found that more than half of the wheat farmers surveyed would try GE wheat if it were available, despite the farmers' own concerns about the possible environmental effects of GE wheat. Only about a quarter of wheat farmers responded that they would not try GE wheat were it available.[17] In addition, the National Association of Wheat Growers (NAWG), one of the most important wheat growers' associations in the US, issued a press release in support of Roundup Ready wheat. For these and other farmers, the appeal of GE crops can be found in their potential to increase yields, reduce pesticide use, preserve topsoil, and ease work toward weed maintenance. Ultimately, however, Monsanto decided in 2004 not to make GE wheat commercially available, despite its investment and research into HT wheat. Importantly, not all farmers subscribe to such benefits from GE crops. In the next section, in fact, I look in depth at farmer opposition to the adoption of GE crops despite such potential benefits. We will also return to the question of why Monsanto decided against releasing GE wheat in the next section.

For agrifood corporations, biotechnology in agriculture has helped to create a new strategy of accumulation, a new pathway for profits. GE crops have also helped to induce social reorganization in agriculture, in the sense that farmers have lost some degree of control over production. Prior to GE crops, farmers would either save seed for the next planting season, or they would buy seed from a seller who was frequently local and in a competitive market. With GE crops, however, farmers must purchase seeds from seed companies that are often global, and farmers must do so on an annual basis. Seed companies hold patents on GE crops, and when farmers save seeds they violate the intellectual property rights of the seed companies holding the patents. In this way, patents on GE crops represent a further commodification of seeds. That is, seeds have increasingly become private property rather than public goods as genetic engineering has progressed. And by issuing patents on GE crops and enforcing intellectual property rights internationally, nation-states and international organizations (e.g., the WTO) have enforced this shift in agriculture, effectively protecting profits for agrifood corporations.

In contrast to farmers and agrifood corporations, consumers currently see little benefit to GE crops. Since most GE crops available today are first generation with a focus on improving elements of production, they do not create clear or obvious benefits for consumers. At best, biotech advocates argue that GE crops do not harm consumers – though this may not be as clear-cut as GE advocates suggest, given the example of StarLink maize, which had the potential to be an allergen. Regardless of whatever concerns US consumers may have about GE foods, they likely eat many products derived from GE crops – particularly, cornmeal, corn syrups, soybean and cottonseed oils – but are largely unaware of their GE origins. Thus, the acceptance of GE crops by consumers, especially those in the US, might be seen as passive: they do not advocate or necessarily even welcome GE crops in the food system, but neither do they oppose GE crops in an overt manner.[18]

If we pause for a moment to focus on farmers, we can see that their decisions about GE crops are quite important. Where farmers resist the adoption of GE crops, this biotechnology is less likely to take hold. Farmers' attitudes toward GE crops are not the single determining factor in the adoption of GE crops, but they are nonetheless important and worth examining closely. Farmers have adopted some GE grains – maize, soybeans, and canola – quite readily in some countries, most notably the US, Brazil, Argentina, and Canada. In each instance, these GE grains are first generation with characteristics focused on production, either pest or weed management, offering farmers some benefits. But, is farmers' adoption of GE crops that simple?

The adoption of GE canola in Canada helps to illustrate the

attraction of biotechnology for some farmers. Monsanto and Bayer CropScience each sell GE canola that is herbicide tolerant (HT) – Roundup Ready and Liberty Link, respectively. HT canola can appeal to farmers on several counts. First, it increases yield by improving the weed management system. Average yield in canola in Canada increased from 1.2 MT per hectare in 1994 to 2.1 MT per hectare in 2015 – an increased yield of 75 percent. Second, the glyphosate-based herbicides are one pass, which reduces the machine operations. Third, HT canola is compatible with zero-till practices that help to conserve topsoil. Emily Eaton outlines some of the ways that HT canola is beneficial for farmers. GE canola brings potential benefits in farm management practices and costs as well as in improved yields (which of course means increased farm incomes), and this is also true for other HT grains.[19]

Of course, this is not to say that GE grains are without negative aspects. First, GE seeds are more expensive than conventional seeds, largely because they are patented. And perhaps more importantly, the patents on GE seeds allow the companies to control farmers' use of GE seeds. Specifically, these seed companies can prevent farmers from saving seeds to use for the next year's crop. Traditionally, many farmers have saved some portion of their harvest to use as seeds in the next planting seasons. Monsanto and Bayer, however, have explicitly prohibited this practice: Monsanto has long prohibited seed saving, and Bayer began prohibiting seed saving in 2005. Monsanto gained some notoriety for suing farmers for saving seeds, including the case *Bowman* v. *Monsanto* in which the US Supreme Court decided unanimously in 2013 that an Indiana farmer, Vernon Hugh Bowman, had violated Monsanto's patent by saving and replanting Roundup Ready (RR) soybeans. Thus, companies can require farmers using these patented GE seeds to purchase new seeds each season. This changed for Monsanto in 2015, however, when the US patent expired for RR soybeans. (In Canada, the patent for RR soybeans expired in 2011.) Monsanto now allows farmers to save RR seeds, assuming that the particular variety of RR is not under another patent (i.e., for the particular variety, separate from the RR gene) but farmers may be able to obtain a license to save the seed. Regardless, Monsanto now sells Roundup Ready 2 Yield soybeans, which have the same gene as RR but it is inserted in a different part of the DNA.

Second, there is a risk of farmers overusing one kind of herbicide – such as a Roundup or Liberty – and contributing to weeds that are resistant to the herbicide.[20] Consequently, farmers growing GE grains may need to use additional herbicides in their weed management systems, thereby eliminating a primary benefit of GE crops: reducing herbicide use. The same is true for effectiveness of GE crops in controlling insect threats. In 2015, in fact, the USEPA proposed limits on the planting of GE maize – either Bt maize or HT/Bt – "to combat a voracious pest that has evolved to resist the bug-killing crops." After more than a decade of expansion in GE maize adoption, corn rootworm has evolved to resist Bt maize and pose a significant pest management problem for US maize farmers.[21]

Third, the production of GE canola made it much more difficult for farmers to produce and market organic canola, which would be bound for the US, EU, and Japan. Canadian farmers began growing GE canola in 1995, and GE canola production spread and reached about 90 percent by the early 2000s. At that point, GE canola had "thoroughly contaminated the canola seed supply and handling system."[22] This created problems for organic canola farmers.

In the end, however, many farmers have decided that the benefits brought by some GE grains outweigh these disadvantages. That is, GE grains have brought benefits in terms of pest control and weed management, as well as crop yields (due in part to reduced losses from insects and weeds). Given the high adoption rates for soybeans, maize, and canola, we might ask why GE food grains have not taken hold. The answer, of course, has to do with strong resistance from various groups, including farmers. But this begs the question of why some farmers resist GE crops, while others embrace them.

Resistance to GE Grains

Resistance to GE grains, and other GE crops, can come from a number of possible sources: consumers, farmers, agrifood corporations, food retailers, environmental activists and organizations, national governments, and even international organizations. And this opposition to GE grains can be based on a variety of claims or concerns, including concerns about food safety, the environment, adequate regulatory oversight, and even economic effects like the market concentration discussed earlier.

Consumers have tended to be resistant to or at least wary of genetically engineered foods, including GE grains. This has been true in the US as well as the EU, even if mobilization has been much weaker in the former than the latter. For example, a 2005 survey of Americans by the Pew Research Center found that half of respondents said that they would oppose the introduction of GE foods into the US food system, and one-third of respondents said that they would strongly oppose GE foods.[23]

What is the root of this resistance? Robert Paarlberg argues that consumers do not see enough benefits from GE crops, which are primarily first generation and have traits focused on the point of production. The benefits of GE crops go primarily to farmers – in the form of reduced use of pesticides or more efficient weed control – and to biotech companies, such as Monsanto, which gain greater control over the production process – through control over seeds – and greater sales of other products, such as herbicides. Since consumers see few benefits from GE crops, they have little incentive to accept them. Other observers argue that there is something unique about food, which people consume daily or even hourly to survive, that makes it different from, say, medicine. Therefore, consumers are likely to resist such extensive use of science and technology in food.[24]

While consumers in both the US and the EU oppose GE crops, GE foods abound in US grocery chains because of the high adoption rate of GE maize and soybeans among US farmers. With over 90 percent of soybean and maize hectares in the US growing GE crops, meat and processed foods in the US are likely to contain genetically engineered ingredients in the form of feed consumed by animals, corn syrup, and oils. Some estimates state that about 70 percent of grocery store items in the US contain genetically engineered ingredients. The pervasiveness of GE foods in the US belies consumers' opposition to such foods. However, US consumers have little knowledge about the use of GE crops in processed foods since the US does not require that products with GE ingredients be labeled as such. Consequently, resistance to GE foods has not gained the same momentum in the US as it has in the EU.

Resistance to GE crops in the EU has waned in influence in recent years, however, as the EU has begun to accept the importation of GE maize and soybeans for food and feed. Beginning in 2004, the EU began to approve GE crops, primarily maize, for use in food and feed. In 2008, the EU approved the first GE soybean. By 2013, the EU had approved dozens of GE crops for import, including many varieties of maize, as well as soybeans and potatoes. In 2015, the EU was importing about 60 GE products, including 32 strains of GE maize and 12 GE soybeans. Thus, about two-thirds of the GE crops that the EU imports are maize or soybeans. This expansion in the GE crops allowed for import under EU regulations was spurred, in large part, by concerns about possible shortages in feed grains in Europe.[25]

This brings us to one more source of resistance: farmers. Some farmers have resisted adopting GE crops. We can see this among wheat farmers, for instance. No GE food grains have become commercially available, although seed companies have developed them. Farmers were part of a broad-based coalition in Canada that organized against GE wheat that also included environmentalists, the Canadian Wheat Board (CWB), and an array of civic organizations (e.g., health organizations and associations of rural local governments). These organizations engaged in lobbying, appeared at legislative hearings, organized public meetings and a mass media campaign, and produced research reports on GE wheat, including its potential effects on individuals' health and the economic well-being of Canadian farmers. Among these tactics, this coalition publicly called for Monsanto to withdraw its application to sell GE wheat in Canada, claiming that it could pose a serious threat to the Canadian wheat industry and to farmers. One survey by the CWB found that 80 percent of farmers would refuse to grow GE wheat. Nonetheless, Andre Magnan – who has studied the Canadian wheat industry, including its opposition to GE wheat – argues that this opposition to GE wheat "is emphatically not a rejection of biotechnology, but born out of a duty to respect the demand of the market."[26]

In addition, some of the opposition in Canada came from organic farmers, with a class-action lawsuit filed against Monsanto by organic canola farmers in 2002. The Saskatchewan Organic Directorate (SOD) filed this suit against Monsanto and Aventis, arguing that the introduction of GE canola led to the loss of organic canola markets. In part, these farmers were concerned with their access to markets in the US, Europe, and Japan. As part of this lawsuit, organic farmers asked for a court injunction against the introduction of GE wheat. In the end, Monsanto decided not to launch commercially the GE wheat it had developed, pulling its GE wheat in 2004.

In France, farmers also organized against GE crops and in a much more dramatic fashion than seen in Canada. The Confederation Paysanne (CP) was the farm organization formed in 1987 that led the opposition to GE crops. The CP reclaimed the title *paysan* ("peasant") in their opposition to industrial agriculture and GE crops, and they identified with international indigenous and peasant organizations and farmers – such as the peasant farmers in Chiapas, Mexico discussed in Chapter 3 and La Via Campesina discussed in Chapters 4 and 6. Jose Bove, a sheep farmer who sold Roquefort milk and cheese, was a leading figure in the formation of the CP and its reclaiming of the *paysan* identity. Bove gained national attention when he dismantled a McDonald's under construction in southern France in 1999, a protest for which he received a three-month prison sentence. The CP launched its campaign against GE crops in 1997, and it used similar high-profile tactics. Most notably, the CP engaged in "crop-pulls" in which anti-GE activists would uproot GE crops in open-air field trials. For example, in 2004 and 2005, CP activists uprooted several Monsanto field trials, and 49 people were arrested. Remarkably, in the trial of those arrested in this crop-pull, the French court sided with the activists because it believed that the government had not fully secured the field trials and protected surrounding agriculture or the public, more generally. Through such public and dramatic actions, then, farmers played a central role in the anti-GE movement in France.[27]

Finally, this same dynamic has led some agrifood corporations to oppose GE grains. We have already seen the resistance by agrifood companies when StarLink entered the food system. A similar example occurred in 2014, when Archer Daniels Midland (ADM) and Cargill each sued Syngenta over lost revenue resulting from China rejecting imports of US maize that contained GE maize produced by the biotech company. Syngenta began to sell maize seeds with a new genetic modification – Agrisure Viptera – to farmers in the US in 2011. Syngenta had won approval from the US, Brazil, and Argentina to allow farmers to grow this GE maize, but China had not approved its import. Then in 2014, the Chinese government rejected shipments of US maize that contained Viptera, resulting in losses of millions of dollars for US maize farmers and grain traders. Consequently, Cargill filed a lawsuit charging that Syngenta had acted irresponsibly in selling Viptera to farmers without first attaining import approval from China. ADM filed its lawsuit two months later, charging that Syngenta had failed to follow its own protocol to prevent contamination in the systems of handling and shipping US maize. Several farmers also filed suits against Syngenta for losses due to the Chinese rejection of US imports and the depressed corn prices in 2014, which were seen as connected to the glut on the world market caused by the import debacle. In 2015, Syngenta filed suit against several grain traders, arguing that those companies should bear the brunt of the burden for the lost imports. These cases are still pending at the time of writing and therefore unresolved, but they highlight the kind of potential divisions among agrifood companies that can affect biotechnology in agriculture.[28]

Importantly, these are divisions regarding GE grains, but they are not exactly examples of agrifood corporations opposing GE crops, in and of themselves. Instead, this is an example of agrifood corporations opposing varieties of GE crops that have not been approved by national governments. If StarLink had been approved for direct human consumption, Kraft may not have balked at it. If the Chinese government had approved

Viptera, Cargill and ADM would not have filed suit against Syngenta. These are examples of how the political context of GE crops can create or exacerbate divisions among agrifood corporations or between producers of different commodities. Nonetheless, these are still examples of how divisions over GE crops can arise among agrifood corporations.

The acceptance of GE grains is not entirely about choices made by farmers and consumers or the weighing of potential costs and benefits. There is also an element of power; there are political-economic factors that also weigh into the acceptance of GM grains. First, let us recall that up to this time, only GE feed grains are commercially available, particularly maize, soybeans, and canola. Second, we can start with the US, where most of the world's GE feed grains are grown. Third, this handful of seed companies has power vis-à-vis farmers through their market control. Robert Falkner notes that, "In 2005, [GE] crops were grown on an estimated 222 million acres around the world, of which Monsanto's [GE] crops were grown on 217.2 million acres, more than 90 percent of the total biotech acreage."[29] In this context, successful resistance to GE grains must involve more than merely deciding not to adopt or not to consume GE crops. Successful resistance – as seen in the examples of food grains – depends on the power to do so, which has meant forging coalitions that include farmers, consumers, and some agrifood companies. The balance of power in food grains favors forces opposed to GE crops, while the balance of power in feed grains favors forces in support of GE crops.

The case of Golden Rice, which is enhanced with vitamin A, helps to demonstrate the potential power of multifaceted resistance. Although Golden Rice was created in 1999, it is not yet commercially available in any country. This may be surprising because, unlike other GE grains, Golden Rice was developed to be freely available rather than to have patent protections enforced for profit. How can we explain why this GE food grain is not available for commercial production? First, Robert Paarlberg notes that complicated legal and patent issues may have slowed down the availability of Golden Rice: "Even though the four most important private companies holding these patents agreed to make them available for Golden Rice on a royalty-free basis . . . the process of bringing this project to commercial completion will be legally complicated."[30] Therefore, even though Golden Rice will not be a proprietary good – or maybe because it will not be a proprietary good – it has been difficult to move it through the regulatory approval process. Second, Syngenta, which obtained the commercial options on Golden Rice in 2001, announced "in 2004 that it had no continuing interest in commercial exploitation of the technology."[31] Third, and perhaps most importantly, Golden Rice has faced vocal opposition in the Philippines, where field tests are being conducted: one morning in the summer of 2013, "400 protesters smashed down the high fences surrounding a field in the Bicol region of the Philippines and uprooted the genetically modified rice plants growing inside."[32] Similar protests against field tests of Bt maize in the Philippines in 2000 and 2001 failed to stop GE maize in the long run, however, as farmers were increasingly planting the GE maize by 2005.[33] Yet, no farmer has adopted Golden Rice some 15 years later. Why would GE rice be different? These three factors – the legal complexity, the corporate hesitancy to act on a food grain, and the protests – certainly all play a role in keeping Golden Rice off the market.

Golden Rice is not the only GE rice, however. Aventis Crop Science, which developed StarLink maize and was later sold to become Bayer CropScience, developed Liberty Link Rice (LLRICE601). After field trials with LLRICE601 under Aventis, Bayer CropScience decided to abandon its pursuit of GE rice in 2001. The StarLink crisis loomed large in this decision. Bayer

CropScience was concerned about losing markets in the EU and Japan if it pursued LLRICE601 and so opted not to seek approval for it. In 2006, however, a company in France found LLRICE601 in the US supply of long grain rice – several years after the research and field trials ended. Marc Gunther, a journalist for *Fortune*, wrote that by the time Bayer CropScience announced the contamination in August 2006, "the tainted rice was everywhere. If [in 2006–7] you or your family ate Uncle Ben's, Rice Krispies, Gerber's, or sushi, or drank a Budweiser –Anheuser-Busch is America's biggest buyer of rice – you probably ingested a little bit of Liberty Link, with the unapproved gene."[34] And Jennifer Clapp notes that this GE rice had permeated the global food system, "By late fall 2006, the environmental group Greenpeace had conducted tests and announced that that LLRICE601 was found in shipments of imported rice in 24 countries, including a significant number of countries in the EU, the Middle East, West Africa, and Asia."[35] In response, the EU banned rice imports from the US; Japan, Iraq, and other countries demanded that the US take steps to improve testing for GE rice and to contain the contamination; and the US told farmers not to plant the effected rice varieties (which were Cheniere and Clearfield 131), which accounted for about 40 percent of US rice plantings. Nonetheless, the US granted regulatory approval to LLRICE601 in November 2006, but Bayer CropScience still faced more than a dozen lawsuits and paid US$750 million to farmers.[36]

Consumer resistance, particularly against GE wheat and rice, has contributed to biotech seed companies abstaining from selling GE food grains. But the world economic context of rice is another important factor. That is, to understand why food grains have been so resistant to commercializing GE while feed grains have shifted heavily toward GE production, we need to look at the world economy and the shape of international grain markets.

Genetically Engineered Grains in the World Economy

Why GE feed grains but not GE food grains? We might argue that consumers find GE feed grains more acceptable than GE food grains. This certainly appears to be true. As we have seen, however, consumers also tend to oppose any GE grains in their food, including in processed foods. Yet, farmers and food companies have been willing to produce and sell GE grains despite such opposition. Looking beyond consumer opposition and how the grain is used, a focus on the world-economic context of grains can shed light on this question.

First, it is worth noting that, in the US, the first GE crops became widely commercially available in 1996. Most discussions note that GE crops became available in the mid-1990s, but they tend not to investigate the timing of commercial GE crops. The commercial release of GE grains coincided with the break with supply management policy in the US, the shift toward liberalization with NAFTA and the WTO, and the acceleration in meat production and consumption. Furthermore, the push to end supply management in the US was driven, in part, by a push by maize producers, who saw demand increasing on the horizon as new markets opened in Russia, Eastern Europe, China, and elsewhere. Global meat consumption continued to increase at a sharp pace, as did the expansion of the processed food industry with its reliance on high fructose corn syrup. In this broad economic context, maize producers could expect that expanding production beyond the limits set by supply management policy would not destabilize market prices or threaten profits since demand for maize was expanding. Consequently, it is also not surprising that feed grain producers may have put forth less resistance to the incorporation of technology – GE seeds – that could further increase their production.

International agreements, particularly those set forth through the WTO, have facilitated the global expansion of seed companies by helping to eliminate national policies that had previously limited intellectual property rights. The WTO's Trade-Related Aspects of Intellectual Property (TRIPS) protects intellectual property rights and covers microorganisms and biological processes for the production of plants, including for biotechnology and patented GE crops, around the world. Biotech agricultural companies had pushed for such international policies that help to privatize seed markets in countries such as Brazil, China, and India. The Cartagena Protocol on Biosafety, which was signed in 2000 and became effective in 2003, provided another opportunity for agrifood corporations to shape rules emerging under liberalization with respect to GE crops. The Cartagena Protocol made a key distinction between organisms meant for release (e.g., seeds) versus commodities (e.g., GE grains), with less stringent regulations on the latter. Furthermore, a WTO ruling in 2006 declared the moratorium on GE crops in the EU to be illegal. This world-economic context was conducive to the global expansion of GE crop production.[37]

Second, another factor that surely cannot be overlooked, but frequently is missing from analyses of GE crops, is the level of competition in world export markets. The US dominates world feed grain exports, and the US and Brazil account for the majority of the world's maize and soybean exports. By contrast, the world food grain markets are more competitive. The international wheat market has no single country that dominates world wheat exports. When the US shifted to GE maize and soybeans, importing countries – the EU, China, and so on – had few places to turn to find conventional feed grains. In 2014, the three largest soybean exporters – Argentina, Brazil, and the US – grew and exported almost exclusively GE soybeans.

If the US shifted to GE wheat, however, importing countries

could turn to one of several other significant wheat exporters – the EU, Canada, Australia, Russia, or a few others. A fear of losing markets, then, was likely a factor in refraining from adopting GE food grains. In fact, rice and wheat farmers made this very point. Since no country grows and exports GE wheat, a shift in that direction could result in losing markets to other countries exporting only conventional wheat. This was a concern for – and in fact, the major argument used by – Canadian farmers resisting GE wheat. Furthermore, one of the world's primary wheat-exporting regions was the EU (particularly, France), which still prohibits the production of GE wheat.[38] This same market context applies to rice: with several exporters of rice, importing countries would find it easy to shift away from one country that grows Golden Rice (LLRICE601). Both the global rice and wheat markets are much more competitive than the markets for feed grains. Furthermore, the market for feed grains differs from those for rice and wheat in that all of the major feed grain exporters have adopted GE crops.

The existing literature on resistance to GE grains acknowledges that export markets play an important role in that resistance, but the emphasis has been on how much a country relies on exports. For example, some observers note that the percent of wheat exported from the US is higher than that for maize – in 2015, about 40 percent and 12 percent, respectively. This logic does not always hold, though. In that same year, Canada exported 50 percent of its canola, which is GE. And the US and Brazil exported high percentages – 43 percent and 57 percent – of the soybeans they produce, which are virtually all GE. Thus, the reliance on exports does not seem to be the determining factor. Instead, the degree of competition in the world market seems a more important factor. Canada accounts for 65 percent of world canola exports; Brazil and the US together accounted for 59 percent of maize exports and 79 percent of soybean exports in 2015. By contrast, five countries accounted for 81 percent of world rice exports, and six countries accounted for 82 percent of world wheat exports. Therefore, the export markets for rice and wheat are much more competitive, and this leads farmers, agrifood corporations, and national governments to resist the adoption of GE food grains.

Finally, we might consider one final difference between food grains and feed grains as contributing to the adoption or rejection of GE seeds: expanding global demand. The global demand for feed grains has increased at a much faster rate than has the demand for food grains. This is, of course, due to the tremendous increase in meat production and consumption discussed in previous chapters. This growing demand for feed grains helped to fuel the preference for and push to supply management policy, expand liberalization and world trade, as well as the adoption of GE varieties of maize and soybeans. And all three of these shifts facilitated a sharp expansion in feed grain production over the past 25 years: maize production increased by more than 100 percent, and soybean production increased by more than 200 percent. By contrast, global wheat production increased by just 25 percent, and rice production increased by 35 percent. The growth in demand for food grains did not compel the adoption of GE varieties. As the next chapter demonstrates, the growing demand for feed grains, in particular, has also had a profound impact on land rights around the world.

CHAPTER SIX

Seeds of Change

This book has focused on political and economic divisions among farmers who produce grains in different regions, agrifood companies that process grains or sell seeds, and countries that export or import grains. Perhaps the most significant division is between food grains and feed grains, especially rice and wheat on the one hand, and maize and soybeans on the other hand. Differences in the use of and market structure for food grains and feed grains can lead to divergent policy preferences regarding government regulations, international trade, and even biotechnology. The political and economic divisions can then contribute to a broad array of social processes. As we have seen, divisions between food and feed grains have contributed to broader trends in national and international policy, such as the activist state of the mid-twentieth century and the liberalization of the world economy over the past 35 years. They have also contributed to economic conflicts over markets, as seen in the trade wars over wheat between the US and the EU, and the eruption of a peasant rebellion in Mexico with the expansion of free trade through NAFTA. These divisions have played a role in world hunger and even influenced the adoption or rejection of biotechnology, as almost all of the GE crops grown in the world are feed grains.

Perhaps the most significant factor contributing to the division between food grains and feed grains has been the expansion in global meat production and consumption, which has meant expanding demand for feed grains and, hence, a substantial increase in the production of maize and soybeans. Feed grain producers, countries that produce feed grains, and agrifood companies in the feed grain industry are likely to see opportunities to expand production and markets in ways that are not so readily available to food grain producers. This division is clearly linked to the global political and economic trends of the past 40 years, which have included more market-oriented policies that allow production to expand, whether through the adoption of biotechnology, the elimination of supply management policy, or the creation of rules allowing for greater international trade.

Along with this greater reliance on the market, we have seen many examples of farmers' resistance since the 1990s, including by the Zapatistas in Mexico, the Confederation Paysanne in France, and farmers in Canada. While some of this opposition was aimed at changing national policies, other opposition was directed at the WTO rules, and still other opposition was directed at the use of biotechnology in agriculture. In some instances, the opposition was successful and gained some concessions, but in other instances it gained little. All of this opposition, however, targeted the emerging global industrial food system centered on market processes, free trade principles, and the incorporation of technology.

The mobilization of political opposition from below has been spurred by recent changes in agriculture in the world economy, especially where grains are concerned. The spread of neoliberal policies and the search for new markets, discussed in Chapter 3, has brought greater instability in the lives of many producers and consumers around the world. For many grain producers, these changes have meant greater economic instability, either in terms of price volatility or access to land. For some grain producers, these policies have meant leaving the land in search of employment in urban centers. For other producers, it has meant adopting new technologies to avoid falling behind in the market. For some consumers, this shift in policies has meant instability in accessing food. For other consumers, the current era has brought questions in terms of the quality of food, such as concerns over the use of GE grains. For many farmers and consumers, these changes have meant confronting agrifood corporations that have grown in size, economic power, and political influence. All of this has played some role in the mobilization from below.

La Via Campesina ("the peasant way") is an organization that emerged in the 1990s in opposition to global trends toward increasing reliance on the market. Via Campesina brings together more than 140 organizations representing farmers and peasants from 73 countries around the world. Responding to trends in industrial agriculture, including GE crops, Via Campesina advocates for the rights of "peasants, small and medium-size farmers, landless people, women farmers, indigenous people, migrants and agricultural workers from around the world."[1] It has brought thousands together to join in protests against organizations like the WTO in Seattle, Cancun, and elsewhere. But Via Campesina is probably best known for its promotion of the idea of food sovereignty, which is the right of people to have access to and control over adequate, healthy, and culturally appropriate food. This has also led Via Campesina and other organizations like it to focus on perhaps the primary resource in the production of grains: land. As the global industrial food system encroaches into areas where the production of grains has been bound by traditions and goals not emphasized by the market, this movement to protect peasants and small farmers against the wave of neoliberalism in the world economy has led to a significant focus on – and therefore some conflict over – control of land. This points to the importance of land and the issue of land reform in the global food system and points of resistance to it.[2]

The preceding chapters have emphasized how the

geopolitics of grains affects shifts in the global food system, economic competition and conflicts between grains, world hunger, and the use of biotechnology in grain production. This closing chapter highlights how the processes outlined and emphasized throughout this book affect people's access to land, which means looking more closely at the effect of the geopolitics of grains on small farmers and peasants represented by organizations such as Via Campesina. As Derek Hall points out in his book *Land*, "The recently intensified state and corporate drive for land for large-scale agriculture . . . [has] fallen especially heavily on indigenous peoples."[3] Not all peasants and small farmers are indigenous peoples, and not all indigenous peoples are peasants or small farmers. Still, there is overlap in these groups regarding the effects of and resistance to the global food system. Turning our attention to land helps to highlight some of the negative, wide-reaching effects of the recent trends in the world economy and how they relate to grains. But examining access to land and the processes of land expropriation and land reform also illuminates some actions and policies that might begin to ameliorate some of the negative effects of the divisions between food grains and feed grains. That is, this discussion might help to highlight how change has happened in the past and how it might happen in the future.

We first turn to the processes of land expropriation and of land reform over the past century. Then, we will see the connections to the divisions between food grains and feed grains that have helped to shape changes in the global food system.

Expropriation of Land, Land Reform, and the Geopolitics of Grains

The geopolitics of grains over the centuries has influenced the relationship between people and land. For indigenous peoples, especially, this relationship has "been marked by centuries of colonialism, racism, displacement, expropriation and/or use of land without indigenous consent."[4] Peasants in various regions of the world – in Africa, Asia, Europe, and Latin America – have experienced an ebb and flow of access to land. At times, they have seen land forcibly taken from them; at other times, powerful peasant movements have contributed to land redistribution that has led to greater rural equality. These periods of divergent land rights are important. In some historical moments, land is expropriated as it becomes a commodity to be bought and sold according to market principles. At other points in history, land is redistributed in a more equitable manner or common ownership of land is re-established through land reform, thereby increasing access for peasants and smallholders.

At their core, land expropriation and land reform involve changes in the distribution of land, as well as the transfer of landownership or property rights from one group to another. This often means changing such things as who can own land and how much land they can own. Prior to incorporation into the world capitalist system, many societies had much land that was held in common, thus allowing the community to have access to it. This access was generally restricted in some way, such as giving each peasant access to some portion of the commons. Other societies regulated access to land through usufruct rights, which allowed people to use land as long as it was not altered in the process. The emergence of the market economy involved privatizing land that had been held in common and regulated by usufruct rights. Such commodification of land usually involved land expropriation and sometimes violence. This process was enforced by political power, with national governments generally enforcing the expropriation of land in some way.

Land reform, by contrast, involves national policies that

provide land to the landless or land-poor, and may re-establish land held in common. Just as with land expropriation, the state plays a central role in land reform, and again like the process of land expropriation, land reform programs entail a change in landownership and property rights. With land reform, however, these changes do not aim to make land a commodity; rather, land reform aims to increase equity in landownership and access to land. Land reform involves the transfer of wealth – in the form of land – from wealthy landowners to poorer peasants, smallholders, or landless peoples. Therefore, state involvement is generally necessary to compel and enforce such transfers of property and changes in land tenure.

Changes in land tenure can involve movement toward market processes and the commodification of land, or the creation of more regulations and limits on privatization. In both cases, the force of the state is involved or even necessary.[5] How can we explain the historical shifts between land expropriation and land reform, and how do these shifts relate to the geopolitics of grains? We can see the answers to these questions in the ebb and flow of expropriation and reform over the past century. These answers help to illustrate the impact of the geopolitics of grains, the split between food grains and feed grains, international food regimes, and how all of these factors can contribute to opportunities for change.

Land Expropriation During the British Food Regime, 1860–1914
The British food regime supported national policies that favored the market economy and aimed to "free the market" to rely on market mechanisms, resulting in the expropriation of land. Sometimes the land expropriation occurred through changing the establishment of private property rights and the consolidation of land through purchases, and other times violence and force played a much more central role in the establishment of private property rights. This is a key element

of the process of "accumulation by dispossession" – that is, accumulating wealth and property by taking it from others. During the British food regime, land expropriation served to consolidate landownership, concentrating land in the hands of a small portion of the population. One example of this is the colonization that took place, especially in Africa and parts of Asia, beginning with the Berlin Conference of 1884. The European powers – Great Britain, the Netherlands, France, Italy, Germany, Spain, and Portugal – colonized almost all of Africa between 1881 and 1914, a period that has been referred to as the "Scramble for Africa." During colonization, traditional systems of land tenure or ownership adhered to by indigenous peoples were dismantled, and land was commodified or confiscated. This expropriation through colonization at the turn of the century provided many resources, including agricultural production, for European colonizers.[6]

Colonization is not the only example of land expropriation that occurred during the British food regime. In Mexico during the mid-1800s, for example, liberal national policies increased the commodification of land. During this period, large haciendas formed and land became concentrated in private hands. In the 1850s, liberals in Mexico pushed for national policies that would facilitate economic development and expand market forces. To this end, the Mexican Constitution of 1857 called for land that had been owned by the Catholic Church or communally by indigenous peoples to be privatized. Not surprisingly, the primary result of these changes in land tenure was increased concentration of land ownership. This period of liberalizing land policies – with land tenure changes aimed at advancing the market economy – lasted from the 1850s to 1910 and resulted in a significant reduction in access to land (more than 90 percent) for indigenous peoples. This was not a period of land reform that helped small farmers or that aimed to enhance food security for the nation or its people.[7]

Along with the colonization of Africa and commodification of land in Mexico and other countries, the British food regime saw a particular type of colonization play an important role: settler colonies that provided grains and meat for Europe. Through settler colonies, imperial powers – Britain, in particular – expropriated land from indigenous peoples and then gave or sold the land to emigrants to settle the area. These settlers in places such as the US, Canada, New Zealand, Australia, South Africa, and Zimbabwe produced grains and meat that were then exported back to Europe. Land expropriation was a cornerstone of the British food regime, and it provided essential resources and food to fuel European industrialization. It also reflected the principle of free trade and expansion of the market economy upon which British hegemony rested. As the world-economic context changed, however, control over land also shifted.[8]

Land Reform During the US Food Regime, 1945–75
Both the British and US food regimes were anchored in grains, particularly wheat. Unlike the British food regime, however, the US food regime rested on extensive regulations in agriculture, as we saw in previous chapters. Whatever its faults, the US food regime offered farmers and peasants around the world some protection against the market economy. This was evident by the global spread of supply management policy, which offered farmers some protection from market vagaries in prices and production and helped to coordinate trade. Another example of such protection came in land reforms, which expanded landownership to include peasants and indigenous peoples who had suffered from the expropriation of their land during the British food regime. Mexico and South Korea provide examples of the process of land reform.

Mexico experienced a second period of land tenure changes following the revolution in 1910. The timing of this revolution is important: it occurred as the British food regime crumbled and during the decline of British hegemony, more generally. In such periods of decline and change in the world economy, there is a possibility of openings for weaker groups in society to assert their demands. In the early 1900s, peasants and others in Mexico seized on this opportunity. The Mexican Revolution in 1910 resulted in political changes that included the reinstitution of common lands and limited land redistribution. Some of the less productive haciendas were broken up and smaller plots of land were redistributed to peasants and other smallholders. These reforms following the revolution, however, tended toward minimal changes aimed at keeping potentially rebellious peasants at bay. The height of Mexican land reform came a few decades later, during the administration of Lazaro Cardenas from 1934 to 1940. Under Cardenas, the national government redistributed 20 million hectares (about 45 million acres) of agricultural land. Importantly, much of the land redistributed under Cardenas was high-quality farmland. This was in contrast to the land redistributed in previous decades, much of which was marginal land with little productive capacity. Furthermore, much of this redistributed land went to reconstitute and expand the ejidos, common land composed of both individual parcels and common spaces to which ejidatarios (ejido members) had access. Notably, the ejidos had been decimated by liberal land reforms in the mid-1800s. In addition to redistributing land, Cardenas also created national policies that supported agricultural production on the ejidos, including greater credit, farm subsidies, and technical assistance. The effect of this land reform was remarkable as landless laborers fell to just 36 percent of the rural labor force, down from 68 percent before the reforms. To help effect this redistribution of land, Cardenas drew on the strength of campesinos (peasants), "by arming more than 60,000 campesinos to defend their land from attacks by the security forces employed by or allied with the affected land-owners."[9] Mexican land reform, then, accelerated just as the US food regime was emerging, and would remain a central part of the Mexican national political and economic landscape until the 1990s.

In the middle of the twentieth century, South Korea also experienced land reform in the direction of protection from the market. The Cold War of the 1940s and 1950s brought a divided Korea, tensions between the Soviet Union and the US, and a new communist threat in China. In particular, the communist regime of North Korea instituted extensive land reforms leading up to its attempt to reunify Korea through the Korean War. With the support of the US, South Korea engaged in land reform that capped landownership at about 3 hectares (7.5 acres). Land redistribution began under the direction of the US military governor, General John R. Hodge, and then was continued by South Korean President Synghman Rhee following the end of the Korean War. This redistribution resulted in the transformation of the traditional landlord class, the yangban, which had long dominated Korean politics and society. The rural change created by land reform was immense: "In 1944, the richest 3 percent of farming households owned 64 percent of all the farmland . . . [but] by 1956, the top 6 percent of households owned only 18 percent [of all farmland]."[10] Remarkably, tenancy dropped from 49 percent to 7 percent of farm households and rice yields more than doubled over the next 20 years. Relative to Mexico, where land reform centered, in part, on re-establishing ejidos and land held in common, land reform in Korea was much more directly aimed at promoting and reinforcing privately held land. Nonetheless, all of this land reform shared the goal of establishing smallholdings and a more equitable distribution of land.[11]

Beyond Mexico and Korea, land reform was widespread

during the US food regime. US military occupation after the Second World War brought land reform to Japan and Taiwan that was similar to Korea's. In all three countries, agricultural production and efficiency improved following the land reforms, which gave farmers a greater stake in the improvements of their land, relative to their interest in land improvements as tenants who only rented land. Land reform also occurred in Germany and southern Italy in the 1940s and 1950s, as "land was widely redistributed in response to peasant militancy."[12] In the 1960s, land reform also swept across Latin America – in Brazil, Chile, Colombia, Costa Rica, the Dominican Republic, Ecuador, Nicaragua, Panama, Peru, and Venezuela. These land reforms varied in their reach, but all of the reforms reshaped political power and redistributed land in these countries.

Land reform can bring several benefits. First, landownership can encourage small cultivators to increase yields and cultivate land more intensively. Second, land reform erases the primary source of discontent in rural areas – land inequity – thereby greatly reducing the likelihood of peasant rebellions. Third, land reform also encourages national economic development by greatly reducing the political power of large landowners, who generally oppose using revenue from rural or agricultural production for industrial or urban development. In short, land reform can contribute to improved agricultural production, political stability, and economic development. All of this was particularly appealing to the US – the world-economic hegemon – against the backdrop of the Cold War, in which the Soviet Union appealed to poorer countries by promoting land reform. The US also supported land reform strategically, as a way to blunt the appeal of the Soviet Union. All of this contributed to the US supporting land reform in Asia, Europe, and Latin America in the mid-twentieth century.

Despite its momentum up to the 1960s and the benefits that it brought, land reform was largely abandoned as a strategy of national development and agrarian policy by about 1975, at the same historical moment that the US food regime declined. The few instances of land reform that occurred at the end of the US food regime, for example in Thailand in 1975, generally were not pursued with any vigor. Consequently, little land was redistributed and concentration of landownership remained largely unchanged. Land reform was tied to the broader agrarian and agricultural policies favored during the US food regime, particularly policies that supported farmers and agricultural development. Therefore, the timing of the demise of land reform should not be a surprise since it was tied to the US food regime in important ways.[13]

Land Reform and Land Expropriation in the Era of
Neoliberalism, 1975 to the Present
Land reform in the middle of the twentieth century, during the US food regime, often reflected the restriction of market processes and generally involved redistribution of land and the re-establishment of commons and usufruct rights. Importantly, food grains, most notably wheat, drove the general framework of this food regime. As this food regime faltered in the 1970s, the center of grains in the world economy shifted to feed grains, as shown in Chapter 3. This shift entailed a change in the substance and aim of land reforms that occurred in the middle of the twentieth century. Whereas proponents of land reform during the US food regime understood the market as an obstacle to efficient land use and ownership, land reform programs after the decline of the food regime tended to be based on the view that the state was the source of land inefficiency. In addition to market-oriented land reforms, the decline of the US food regime also eventu-

ally brought a return of land expropriation, in the form "land grabs" or large land acquisitions.

The land reforms that have occurred under neoliberalism tend to differ from those in the mid-twentieth century by aiming to rely on market processes. The approach of market-led agrarian reform (MLAR) involves land redistribution through market processes, that is, through the purchasing and selling of land. MLAR programs generally provide peasants or indigenous peoples with some funds with which they can purchase land at market prices. In part, the idea is to use market-oriented processes and refrain from confiscation and redistribution by the national government. Other market-oriented reforms have commodified communal or public lands that previously were not alienable, that is not available for sale or purchase.

One example of MLAR occurred in South Africa, which began its process of land reform after democratization in 1994. As the African National Congress (ANC) first outlined its proposals for land reform in 1992, it advocated government confiscation and purchase of lands for redistribution. Over the next few years, however, the spread of neoliberalism in the world economy – through the WTO, various free trade agreements, and the influence of the World Bank and IMF – contributed to the adoption of MLAR with the idea of "willing buyer, willing seller" at the center of the policy. In the 1990s, the land reform policies focused on aiding poor households, but since 2001, the focus of reforms has been on commercial farmers. In particular, the land reform program now offers larger grants but requires beneficiaries to make contributions based on the size of the grant. This policy, then, tends to favor those who already have resources. Perhaps more importantly, the reform program gives landowners a veto through "the freedom to negotiate their own price which should, in theory, be market-based or market equivalent."[14] At any rate, land reform in South Africa has consistently fallen short of its goals: in 1994, "a target for the entire land reform programme [was] to redistribute 30% of this within a five-year period. . . [but] by 2006 only 4.1% of agricultural land had been transferred."[15] Thus, the MLAR in South Africa looks quite distinct from the land reforms during the US food regime, both in terms of process and outcomes.

The World Bank has tended to favor this style of land reform. For example, Brazil received a US$90 million loan from the World Bank in 1997 to implement a pilot MLAR program. Brazil used this loan to provide low-income rural producers with loans of up to US$40,000 to help with land purchases. The World Bank's support for MLAR as the preferred style of land reform can also be seen in its evaluation of the Philippines' Comprehensive Agrarian Reform Program (CARP), which was passed in 1988 and limited landownership to 5 hectares, with an additional 3 hectares for each heir. Landlords, including President Corazon Aquino, whose family owned a 6,400-hectare sugar plantation, resisted this policy. Despite this opposition, CARP showed moderate success in land redistribution, especially between 1992 and 2000. The World Bank, however, expressed caution about the viability of the land redistribution component of CARP, arguing that it would result in average farm sizes too small to be competitive in the market. The World Bank further warned, "CARP must not undermine the functioning of land markets as they are the most effective way to redistribute agricultural land from less to more efficient producers and at the same time open the agricultural ladder to landless household."[16] Thus, the emphasis of MLAR as favored by the World Bank is, again, "willing buyer, willing seller." Land reform in the Philippines moved in this direction after 2000.

In the period of liberalism after 1975, we can see a different version of market-oriented land reforms in Mexico. In 1991,

the Mexican Constitution was amended to end land redistribution, to allow ejidatarios "the right to sell, rent, sharecrop,
or mortgage their individual parcels and to enter into joint
ventures and contracts with private (including foreign) investors and stockholding companies," and also to allow "the
collective right of ejidatarios to dissolve the ejido and distribute the property among members."[17] In contrast to Brazil, the
Philippines, and South Africa, then, market-oriented land
reform in Mexico was not about using the market to redistribute land that was privately held. Instead, the reforms in
Mexico were about allowing ejidos to be privatized. This set of
policy changes was a response to NAFTA and the push by US
maize producers and the feed grain industry to gain access to
the market in Mexico. We have already seen the consequences
of these changes to the ejidos: the Chiapas rebellion, which
was discussed in Chapter 3.

Another example of land reform aimed at expanding
market processes can be seen in China. For much of the
past 35 years, economic development has been based on an
expansion of industry that relied on a large low-wage labor
force. Wages in China were lower than its global competitors,
including countries like Mexico and Taiwan. Chinese industry
could pay its workers globally cheap wages because the traditional system of social support gave laborers access to plots of
land in their home villages. These small plots of land helped
workers to subsist, and the system subsidized cheap wages
in China's industrial sector. With continued urban expansion over the past two decades, however, this system of rural
land subsidizing workers has broken down as the expropriation of rural land has increased. Local governments, which
have been in a fiscal crunch for several years, have found land
dispossession to be a source of revenue. Local governments
are able to make money from dispossessions by leasing land
for urban expansion. One primary result is that workers and

their families have lost access to this source of supplemental support, and farming families have lost access to their land. Yet this form of rural land expropriation has fueled the urban construction boom in China, which has been an important source of Chinese economic growth in recent years. The construction industry in China relies on both low-wage labor and cheap land (e.g., through dispossession) for profitability. This accumulation by dispossession mirrors the process of accumulation and economic growth found with colonization. Even a country with recent socialist roots shows land reform tendencies that reflect the trends in the broader world economy: land reform is aimed at further economic growth, urbanization, and industrialization, with the important consequences of furthering inequality and undermining smallholders and peasants.[18]

Finally, "land grabs" represent another example of shifts in land occurring under neoliberalism, and they entail large-scale purchases of land – sometimes hundreds of thousands of hectares at a time – by national governments, financial investment groups, or transnational corporations. Three examples from 2011 help to illustrate some of the larger land grabs. First, the Al-Khorayef Group of Saudi Arabia signed a US$400 million contract with a provincial government in Argentina to gain the rights for 200,000 hectares of farmland to produce food for the Saudi market. Second, the Alberta Investment Management Company, one of the largest pension fund managers in Canada, entered a joint venture to purchase 252,000 hectares in Australia to use for a mix of forestry and agricultural production. And third, Madabeef, a company owned by investors in the UK, acquired 200,000 hectares in Madagascar to use for beef production. The global food crisis of 2008, discussed in Chapter 4, was an important impetus for the recent wave of land grabs, as rising prices for land and agricultural commodities made them appealing targets for

capital investment. At the same time, some national governments have sought food security by purchasing farmland in
other countries.[19]

The shifts in international food regimes have driven
changes in access to land. As a food regime relies more on
market processes, such as during the British food regime
and since the decline of the US food regime, access to land
decreases. The accumulation by dispossession through the
commodification of land in the 1800s reduced the access to
land of indigenous peoples and peasants. The same has been
true of the neoliberal shift since the fall of the US food regime.
Only during the shift toward national regulation and protection from the extremes of the market economy during the US
food regime (1945–75) did access to land increase for such
groups through land reform policies such as redistribution.

How does the ebb and flow of land reform and expropriation relate to the geopolitics of grains and issues such as
world hunger and the adoption of biotechnology? These are
important questions, and the answers help us to get at some
of the deep, fundamental geopolitics of grains. The ebb and
flow of land reform and expropriation relate to the geopolitics
of grains through the international food regimes, which can
create an opportunity for land reform. There is little debate
that wheat was central to both the British and US food regimes
– and it has remained a central agricultural commodity since
the decline of the US food regime after 1975. Nonetheless,
that central position does not necessarily equate to meaning
that wheat was or is the dominant grain politically. During the
British food regime, for example, wheat did not set the parameters. Recall from Chapter 1 that the free trade basis of the
British food regime was supported not by wheat growers in
Britain but rather by livestock producers who favored cheaper
grains. A division existed within British agriculture as the
first food regime formed: wheat producers sought protections

from the market but livestock producers favored market processes over regulation.[20]

During the US food regime, by contrast, wheat was the
politically dominant grain and had a central role in setting
the parameters of the regime, which centered on supply
management and extensive national and international regulation. A division existed in the US between maize producers
and wheat producers, with the former opposing and the latter
favoring supply management policy. Through a coalition with
cotton producers, wheat producers were politically dominant
and set the parameters of the US food regime.[21]

Most recently, the decline of the US food regime came with
a political shift in agriculture: feed grains once again asserted
their dominance over food grains. The continued expansion
of global meat consumption created a set of economic interests in the feed grains sector that contributed to its support for
liberalization of agriculture in the world economy, including
the incorporation of previously protected land into the global
system of industrial agriculture. To whatever extent food grain
producers in the US, Canada, Australia, the EU, and elsewhere might favor policies that provide some protection from
market vagaries, they do not currently have the political power
to set the food regime to reflect such preferences.

In this way, then, the political and economic divisions
between grains have contributed to the likelihood of land
reform. The two periods dominated by feed grains have seen
greater frequency of land expropriations and greater resistance
to substantial land reform. During the British food regime
and the period following the decline of the US food regime,
international trade expanded in a way that was conducive to
land expropriation rather than land reform. These periods
saw trade expansion rest on policies that promoted market
processes. National regulations and traditional constraints
on land, especially commonly held or publicly held land,

could be loosened in such a global context, thereby allowing large sections of land to be incorporated into the global food system. During the British food regime, this was frequently land expropriated to grow wheat. More recently, much of the land expropriated is focused on feed grain production. What is produced on the land is in some ways secondary to the impetus behind the policies that contributed to a context in which expropriation was more likely.

By contrast, the period during which food grains were politically dominant allowed for and even encouraged national and international policies that provide protection against the market – including land reform. International trade during the US food regime relied much more on coordination and regulation. This type of policy contributed to a context in which land reform policies were much more possible, as they fit more closely with the overarching rules of the regime.

There are also clear ways in which land reform and expropriation connect to the issues of world hunger, food security, and the adoption of biotechnology. First, land reform has been shown to reduce hunger and, at the same time, enhance food security. The land reforms in Asia after 1945 led to increases in agricultural productivity, national food security, and rural equality. In addition, rural poverty was reduced. Land reforms in Mexico during the 1930s had similar effects. By contrast, land expropriation has tended to undermine food security. The neoliberal reforms in Mexico during the 1990s have contributed to increased rural poverty and reduced household food security, which has contributed to migration out of the rural areas. Second, land reform and expropriation can be linked to biotechnology and grains, as well. In Argentina and Brazil, for example, the widespread adoption of GE soybeans has contributed to the expansion of industrial agricultural production. This expansion has, at times, occurred by encroaching on public lands, indigenous lands, or commons.

At its outset, this book posed a question: Why did the production of grains increase so substantially over the past 25 years? Table 1.1 showed that maize production, in particular, increased tremendously – doubling between 1990 and 2015, from 481 MMT to 967 MMT. Land expropriation and MLAR, together with the widespread adoption of GE maize, facilitated this sharp rise in global maize production. Furthermore, this increased production, land expropriation, and adoption of GE maize were driven to a great extent by expanding meat production and consumption – the growing need to have more land to grow more grain to feed more animals that would be slaughtered for meat.

The Geopolitics of Grains: Looking Backward, Looking Forward

The influence of grains in politics, economics, culture, and other aspects of society is nothing new. Grains – especially maize, rice, and wheat – have been influential for millennia. This book has shown how, over the past several decades, grains have influenced a variety of social processes: shifts in the global food system, economic competition and conflicts, world hunger, the use of biotechnology, and access to land. Farmers and their organizations, governments, international organizations, and corporations have acted on these issues in ways that reflect their economic interests. Wheat farmers in France and in Canada pushed for price supports, maize farmers in the US and soybean farmers in Brazil adopted GE seeds, the WTO has pushed for greater liberalization of agriculture in the world economy, governments in Australia and South Korea resisted attempts at global liberalization, peasants in Mexico and landless people in Brazil protested for greater support and access to land, and ADM and Cargill each sued Syngenta over the export of GE maize to China.

Importantly, then, grains are not a unitary force in politics or economics and part of the influence of grains has emanated from the divisions between them.

One division that has appeared over and over again is between food grains and feed grains. The differences in the use of grains have repeatedly been influential in a number of issues over the past 80 years, and especially most recently. As Chapter 2 discussed, food grains, in particular wheat, helped to set the US food regime based on supply management policy, which offered some regulation of the market and some protection from market instability. This policy became a central part of rice production in many countries, including Japan, South Korea, and India. During this time, the US was the world's leading feed grains producer and accounted for the majority of the world's maize and soybean exports. While maize and soybeans were subject to supply management policy in the US, farmers of these feed grains tended to oppose this policy, regularly seeking to weaken or even eliminate it. This division contributed to the decline of the US food regime and the shift to a more liberal world economy, as seen in Chapter 3, but it was not the only division among grains to contribute to liberalization. The spread of export subsidies in the 1970s and 1980s increasingly put wheat producers in some nations at odds with those in other nations. In fact, the escalation in the use of export subsidies was a primary factor leading to the formation of the Cairns Group – which included Argentina, Australia, Brazil, Canada, Indonesia, the Philippines, South Africa, and Vietnam, among others. These agricultural exporting countries sought to end the growing subsidies paid to farmers and grain traders by the US and EU. These shifts in the interests of grains – feed grain farmers and organizations that increasingly opposed production restrictions imposed by supply management policy, wheat-exporting countries that had favored supply management policy for decades pushing for trade reform, and economic conflicts over trade between the US and Europe – all contributed to shifting political power and changes in the global food system. Divisions between grains and the shifts in the economic inter-ests and political power of producers of different grains or in different countries underlie the decline of the US food regime and the consequent global liberalization of agriculture. This liberalizing shift has contributed to further divisions and con-flicts among grains, from the Chiapas rebellion to continued fights over WTO policies to the food riots across the globe in 2007 and 2008. It has also fueled the expansion of global meat production.

The geopolitics of grains does not only shape national poli-cies and international trade, but it also influences important issues of world hunger and biotechnology in agriculture, as Chapters 4 and 5 demonstrated. In fact, the consequences of the divisions between grains already mentioned, particularly the liberalization of agriculture, contributed in particular ways to both world hunger and the patterns of adoption of bio-technology in grains. Therefore, the economic interests and political power of competing grains are central to understand-ing these issues.

The end of the US food regime and its central policy of supply management – which was driven, in part, by the growth of feed grains and increased competition between grains around the globe – resulted in remarkable instabil-ity in world grain markets, for example in world prices. In this context, the global food crisis of 2008 can be seen as an extreme case of the instability and volatility that have charac-terized the market since the decline of the US food regime. But even outside of moments of crisis, as Chapter 4 showed, the general world-economic context shapes the flow of grains and the patterns of production in ways that can contribute to hunger and food insecurity. This was evident even in the

1800s, when the flow of grains out of India, Brazil, and other countries continued despite widespread famine. It continues more recently as food-insecure countries like Pakistan exported food grains even as hunger increased in 2008. And finally, the expansion of meat production and feed grains production has occurred in countries where food insecurity and hunger are pressing issues, most notably India, which is now the world's leading exporter of beef despite being food insecure. The geopolitics of grains draws our attention to the question, for whom are grains produced? In many instances, grains are produced to yield the highest returns, such as through exports or as feed for animals to be slaughtered for meat. Feeding those who suffer from hunger is generally not nearly as profitable.

The geopolitics of grains, the divisions between them, and the liberalization of agriculture over the past 40 years have all shaped the patterns of adopting or rejecting biotechnology. The expansion in global meat production was tied to the push to end supply management, which restricted production. This expanded meat production increased the demand for feed grains. Not only did this create the potential for competition between feed grains and food grains, but it was also one factor contributing to the adoption of GE seeds in feed grain production. As Chapter 5 demonstrated, the varying contexts of grains in the world economy also shaped the adoption of GE seeds. The world markets for rice and wheat are much more competitive than the markets for maize and soybeans. Not surprisingly, then, farmers and agrifood corporations have been more resistant to GE food grains for fear of losing markets. Food grain producers and their national governments have been unwilling to take the risk of adopting GE seeds. Adopting GE maize and soybeans, by contrast, is a "safer bet" in terms of maintaining markets since there are fewer exporters of these feed grains. Here again, the geopolitics of grains is important in understanding the patterns of adopting or resisting biotechnology in agriculture.

The influence of grains does not stop there. Grains also contribute to some of the leading political issues of the day, such as climate change and immigration. The modern global food system accounts for almost one-third of greenhouse gas emissions, thereby constituting a major driver of climate change. The food system contributes to climate change primarily through CO_2 and methane emissions, and this happens through the use of machinery using fossil fuels, chemical fertilizers and pesticides, clear-cutting of forests, and especially livestock production. As previous chapters have argued, the expansion in meat production is tied to feed grains and the push for liberalization in the world economy over the past decades. The opportunities to expand production through increased meat production and consumption were a central factor driving feed grain producers to support liberalization and the end of supply management policy. Grains, then, are an important force in climate change, especially to the extent that feed grains are linked to the expanding meat industry.[22]

Similarly, grains have played a role in international immigration over the past several decades. Via Campesina has argued that the "massive movement of food around the world is forcing an increased movement of people."[23] The case of Mexico provides a clear example. As the feed grains sector won greater liberalization through international agreements such as NAFTA, many small maize producers in Mexico found their livelihoods threatened by increased grain exports from the US and greater market instability. Other crops – in this particular case, coffee – were also increasingly subject to liberalization and market instability. This market instability led many peasants and small farmers or members of their family to leave the land in search of employment in urban areas, including in the US. Phil McMichael notes, "the FAO estimated, conservatively, that 20–30 million peasants were displaced in the 1990s following the institution of the WTO, and in Mexico upward of two million campesinos lost land through the destabilizing impacts of NAFTA."[24] Though we tend to overlook their role, grains have played an important role in international migration through their connection to changes in the global food system – including liberalization, expanding meat production, world hunger, biotechnology, land reform, and climate change.

Given how the geopolitics of grains is connected to so many leading issues of the day, we should not expect the importance of grains to dissipate any time soon. In fact, we should expect the opposite: grains will remain a central political and economic force on a variety of issues. Furthermore, divisions between grains – especially food grains and feed grains – will continue to be important. The conflicts between food grains and feed grains have been fundamentally important to the shifts in the global food system over the past century, and there are few signs that these conflicts will become any less influential in the future.

The politics of grains entails more than merely what kinds of grains we eat, how much of them we eat, in what form we eat them, or even where the grains are produced. It is more complex than the visible battles between farmers, consumers, and large agrifood corporations. To really get at the underlying politics of grains, we need to recognize the conflicts based in geography, we need to examine the political and economic divisions between different grains, and we need to acknowledge the dynamic processes in the world economy that contribute to the ebb and flow of such divisions and conflicts. Within that broader world-economic and historical context, we see much more of the political and economic complexity that lies beneath our abundant choices of food in the super-market. The geopolitics of grains helps to explain shifts in the global food system, economic competition and conflicts, world hunger, the use of biotechnology, access to land, as well as climate change and international migration. Grains funda-mentally shape the political and economic context in which we live.

Notes

1 GRAINS FOR FOOD, GRAINS FOR FEED

1. In this book, I use the term "maize" rather than "corn." While "corn" is commonly used in the US and a few other countries to refer to this particular grain, other people around the world use the term "corn" to refer to grains in general and use "maize" to refer to the particular grain. In addition, "maize" is generally used in international discussions. The Food and Agriculture Organization (FAO) of the United Nations, for example, uses "maize" to refer to the specific grain. Given this book's aim to present a global focus, using "maize" seems most appropriate.

2. Specter, Michael (2014), "Against the Grain: Should You Go Gluten-Free?" *The New Yorker*, November 3, available at www.newyorker.com/magazine/2014/11/03/grain; Wong, Venessa (2011), "Rice: The Secret Ingredient in Everything from Baby Food to Beer," *Bloomberg Business*, March 31, available at http://www.bloomberg.com/bw/lifestyle/content/mar2011/bw20110331_321593.htm; Pollan, Michael (2006), *The Omnivore's Dilemma*, New York: Penguin Press. For more on the link between grains and the fast food industry, see Baines, Joseph (2014), "Food Price Inflation as Redistribution: Towards a New Analysis of Corporate Power in the World Food System," *New Political Economy* 19(1): 79–112, especially pp. 95–6.

3. For a couple of examples of the cultural influence of grains, see Marton, Renee (2014), *Rice: A Global History*, Chicago: Reaktion Books; and Boutard, Anthony (2012), *Beautiful Corn: America's Original Grain from Seed to Plate*, Gabriola Island, BC: New Society Publishers.

4. The statistics found in this book tend to come from the Foreign Agricultural Service (FAS) of the United States Department of Agriculture (USDA), which has the "Production, Supply, &

Distribution (PS&D) Online Database," or the Food and Agriculture Organization (FAO) of the UN, which has "FAOSTAT." Each of these databases is easy to find online at the website of their respective organizations.

5. For discussions on how each of these grains has shaped nations and the world, see Bray, Francesca (1986), *The Rice Economies: Technology and Development in Asian Societies*, New York: Basil Blackwell; Morgan, Dan (1980), *Merchants of Grain*, New York: Penguin Books; and Warman, Arturo (2003), *Corn and Capitalism: How a Botanical Bastard Grew to Global Dominance*, Chapel Hill: The University of North Carolina Press.

6. A large literature exists on the global food crisis of 2008. A few examples include Bello, Walden (2009), *The Food Wars*, London: Verso Books; Holt-Gimenez, Eric, and Patel, Raj (2009), *Food Rebellions! Crisis and the Hunger for Justice*, Oxford: Pambazuka Press; Clapp, Jennifer, and Cohen, Marc J. (eds.) (2009), *The Global Food Crisis: Governance Challenges and Opportunities*, Waterloo, ON: Wilfrid Laurier University Press; Patel, Raj (2012), *Stuffed and Starved: The Hidden Battle for the World Food System* (revised and updated), New York: Melville House Books; McMichael, Philip (2009), "The World Food Crisis in Historical Perspective," *Monthly Review* 61(3): 32–47; Weis, Tony (2013), "The Meat of the Global Food Crisis," *Journal of Peasant Studies* 40(1): 65–85; and Winders, Bill (2012), "The Food Crisis and the Deregulation of Agriculture," *Brown Journal of World Affairs* 18(1): 83–95.

7. On the economic activities of the ABCDs, see Clapp, Jennifer (2015), "ABCD and Beyond: From Grain Merchants to Agricultural Value Chain Managers," *Canadian Food Studies* 2(2): 126–35, p. 126. See also Murphy, Sophia, Burch, David, and Clapp, Jennifer (2012), *Cereal Secrets: The World's Largest Grain Traders and Global Agriculture*, Oxford: Oxfam Research Reports; Howard, Philip H. (2016), *Concentration and Power in the Food System: Who Controls What We Eat?*, London: Bloomsbury; Clapp, Jennifer, and Fuchs, Doris (2009), "Agrifood Corporations, Global Governance, and Sustainability: A Framework for Analysis," pp. 1–26 in *Corporate Power in Global Agrifood Governance*, edited by Jennifer Clapp and Doris Fuchs, Cambridge, MA: The MIT Press.

8. For critical discussions of the global meat industry and its

effects, see Weis, Tony (2013), *The Ecological Hoofprint: The Global Burdens of Industrial Livestock*, New York: Zed Books; and Nibert, David (2013), *Animal Oppression and Human Violence: Domesecration, Capitalism, and Global Conflict*, New York: Columbia University Press.

9. This perspective draws on world system theory, which focuses on the interstate system and the international division of labor in the world economy. Wallerstein, Immanuel (1974), *The Modern World-System I: Capitalist Agriculture and the Origins of the European World-Economy in the Sixteenth Century*, New York: Academic Press, Inc.; and Arrighi, Giovanni (1994), *The Long Twentieth Century: Money, Power and the Origins of Our Times*, London: Verso Books. For a clear demonstration of how agriculture fits in the dynamics of the world system, see Rubinson, Richard (1978), "Political Transformation in Germany and the United States," pp. 39–73 in *Social Change in the Capitalist World Economy*, edited by Barbara Hockey Kaplan, Beverly Hills: Sage.

10. Winders, Bill (2009), *The Politics of Food Supply: U.S. Agricultural Policy in the World Economy*, New Haven, CT: Yale University Press; Winders, Bill, Heslin, Alison, Ross, Gloria, Weksler, Hannah, and Berry, Seanna (2016), "Life After the Regime: Market Instability with the Fall of the U.S. Food Regime," *Agriculture and Human Values* 33: 73–88.

11. See especially, *The Economist* (2011), "The 9 Billion People Question: A Special Report on Feeding the World," February 26; and Conway, Gordon (2012), *One Billion Hungry: Can We Feed the World?*, Ithaca, NY: Cornell University Press.

12. There is a large literature on food regimes. See Friedmann, Harriet (1982), "The Political Economy of Food: The Rise and Fall of the Post-War International Food Order," *American Journal of Sociology* 88(Supplement): S248–S286; Friedmann, Harriet (1993), "The Political Economy of Food: A Global Crisis," *New Left Review* 197: 29–57; McMichael, Philip (2009), "A Food Regime Geneology," *Journal of Peasant Studies* 36(1): 139–69; Pechlaner, Gabriela, and Otero, Gerardo (2010), "The Neoliberal Food Regime: Neoregulation and the New Division of Labor in North America," *Rural Sociology* 75(2): 179–208; and Winders, Bill (2009), "The Vanishing Free Market: The Formation and Spread of the British and US Food Regimes," *Journal of Agrarian Change* 9(3): 315–44.

13. Polanyi's work has become classic material in this kind of political economic and global analysis. Beyond his argument about the double movement, Polanyi's book makes four central arguments: (1) the market economic is socially constructed, not a "natural" outgrowth of individual human characteristics, (2) the contemporary market economy is best understood as a global economy, not independent "national economies," (3) commodification is a central process in the market economy, and the commodification of land, labor, and money are particular points of contestation, and (4) the national state plays a central role in the spread of the market, frequently through the use of force. Each of the points can be found in my analysis of the geopolitics of grains. Polanyi, Karl (1944/2001), *The Great Transformation: The Political and Economic Origins of Our Time*, Boston: Beacon Press.

2 GRAINS AND THE US FOOD REGIME

1. Other scholars identify different starting and ending points of these food regimes. Food regimes represent periods of stability when the patterns of national policy and of international trade are clearly established. The beginning and end of the food regimes are periods of transition, however, that show some signs of change in policies, trade flows, production patterns, consumptions patterns, and so forth. Bigger and more noticeable changes occur as the food regime breaks down. The transition periods tend to be much less stable, and even somewhat chaotic, leading to the possibility of different designations for the time boundaries of food regimes. For example, see Friedmann, Harriet, and McMichael, Philip (1989), "Agriculture and the State System: The Rise and Decline of National Agricultures, 1870 to the Present," *Sociologia Ruralis* 29(2): 93–117; Winders, "The Vanishing Free Market," op. cit.
2. Statistics on British wheat imports come from Mitchell, B.R. (1988), *British Historical Statistics*, Cambridge: Cambridge University Press, p. 224. Mitchell's wheat import statistics are presented in hundredweight (cwt), but I converted them into metric tons.
3. For more detailed discussions of the formation and spread of the British food regime, see Winders, "The Vanishing Free

Market," op. cit. On the divisions between grain and livestock producers in Britain, see McKeown, T.J. (1989), "The Politics of Corn Law Repeal and Theories of Commercial Policy," *British Journal of Political Science* 19(3): 353–80.

4. Statistics on wheat production come from the USDA, *Agricultural Statistics, 1941*, table 5, p. 15.

5. Bray, Francesca (1989), *The Rice Colonies: Technology and Development in Asian Societies*, New York: Basil Blackwell, p. 129.

6. Baker, Christopher (1981), "Economic Reorganization and the Slump in South and Southeast Asia," *Comparative Studies in Society and History* 23(3): 325–49, p. 341.

7. Bray, *The Rice Colonies*, op. cit., p. 129.

8. For statistics, see USDA, *Agricultural Statistics, 1941*, table 138, p. 108. This publication gives imports and exports of rice in pounds and may convey the magnitude of the change a little more clearly. Average annual rice imports for Japan fell from 961 million pounds for 1925–9 to 122 millions for 1930–4.

9. For a more complete discussion of the experience of rice-producing countries in Asia during the Great Depression, see ch. 4 in Latham, A.J.H. (1998), *Rice: The Primary Commodity*, New York: Routledge.

10. USDA, *Agricultural Statistics, 1941*, table 51, p. 51.

11. Latham, *Rice*, op. cit., p. 29.

12. The quotations about GATT come from Dam, Kenneth (1970), *The GATT: Law and International Organization*, Chicago: University of Chicago Press, pp. 27 and 258.

13. Farnsworth, Helen C. (1956), "International Wheat Agreements and Problems, 1948–1956," *Quarterly Journal of Economics* 70: 217–48, p. 217.

14. Information on the IRC comes from the FAO website: www.fao. org/agriculture/crops/thematic-sitemap/theme/treaties/irc/en/. See also Tran, D.V. (2000), "Historical Development, Functions and Achievements of the International Rice Commission since 1949," *International Rice Commission Newsletter*, vol. 49, available at www.fao.org/docrep/x7164t/x7164t11.htm.

15. Sheingate, Adam D. (2001), *The Rise of the Agricultural Welfare State: Institutions and Interest Group Power in the United States, France, and Japan*, Princeton, NJ: Princeton University Press; Anderson, Kym, and Hayami, Yujiro (1986), *The Political*

Economy of Agricultural Protection: East Asia in International Perspective, Boston: Allen & Unwin.

16. Winders, *The Politics of Food Supply*, op. cit., p. 139.
17. Anderson and Hayami, *Political Economy of Agricultural Protection*, op. cit., pp. 64–5. On the one hand, we might say that this combination of price supports and production controls undermined the primary function of this policy: managing the supply of agricultural commodities. That is, we might view this overproduction as a sign that the policy was, therefore, unsuccessful at managing supply because it actually encouraged farmers to produce more grains and other commodities. And, that would be a fair conclusion. On the other hand, the overproduction and resulting surpluses helped to even out supply and stabilize grain markets. Surpluses were used to create grain reserves that were released onto markets during shortfalls in production. Thus, the unintended consequence of encouraging overproduction actually helped to achieve the intended consequence of stabilizing markets. In this way, the policy did, indeed, help to manage supply but not exactly in the way originally intended, which was to prevent surpluses. Instead, the policy managed supply in a way to avoid or overcome significant shortfalls in production and help prevent periodic spikes in commodity prices.
18. Yoon, Byeong-Seon, Song, Won-Kyu, and Lee, Hae-jin (2013), "The Struggle for Food Sovereignty in South Korea," *Monthly Review* 65(1): 56–62, p. 57.
19. Otsuka, Keijiro and Hayami, Yujiro (1986), "Revealed Preference in Japan's Rice Policy," pp. 63–90 in *The Political Economy of Agricultural Protection: East Asia in International Perspective*, edited by Kym Anderson and Yujiro Hayami, Sydney: Allen & Unwin, p. 65.
20. Winders, *The Politics of Food Supply*, op. cit.

3 THE SEARCH FOR NEW MARKETS

1. Healy, Stephen, Pearce, Richard, and Stockbridge, Michael (1998), *The Implications of the Uruguay Round Agreement on Agriculture for Developing Countries: A Training Manual*, Rome: FAO, p. 6.
2. Sheingate, *The Rise of the Agricultural Welfare State*, op. cit., pp. 223–4.

3. Ibid., p. 231.
4. Libby, Ronald T. (1992), *Protecting Markets: U.S. Policy and the World Grain Trade*, Ithaca, NY: Cornell University Press, p. 49.
5. Baines, Joseph (2015), "Fuel, Feed, and the Corporate Restructuring of the Food Regime," *Journal of Peasant Studies* 42(2): 295–321, p. 299.

4 FEED GRAINS, FOOD GRAINS, AND WORLD HUNGER

1. Walt, Vivienne (2008), "The World's Growing Food-Price Crisis," *Time* February 27, available at www.time.com.
2. Schneider, Mindi (2008), " 'We are Hungry!': A Summary Report of Food Riots, Government Responses, and States of Democracy in 2008," available at http://rajpatel. org/2009/11/02/we-are-hungry-exclusive/.
3. FAO (2015), *State of Food Insecurity in the World, 2015: Meeting the 2015 International Hunger Targets: Taking Stock of Uneven Progress*, Rome: Food and Agriculture Organization of the United Nations, p. 52.
4. For more on the global food crisis, see Bello, *The Food Wars*, op. cit.; Holt-Gimenez, and Patel, *Food Rebellions!*, op. cit.; Clapp, and Cohen, *The Global Food Crisis*, op. cit.
5. The "prevalence of undernourishment" has been criticized as being too stringent because it rests on the premise of lower calorie needs (a "sedentary lifestyle") and focuses on episodes of hunger that last for a year or more. Some scholars point out that using the measure the "prevalence of food inadequacy" corrects for these shortcomings and puts the estimate of world hunger in 2012 at about 1.3 billion, which is substantially above the FAO estimate of 868 million for that year using the "prevalence of undernourishment" measure. See Lappe, Frances Moore, Clapp, Jennifer, Anderson, Molly, Broad, Robin, Messer, Ellen, Pogge, Thomas, and Wise, Timothy (2013), "How We Count Hunger Matters," *Ethics & International Affairs* 27(3): 251–9.
6. FAO, *State of Food Insecurity in the World, 2015*, op. cit., p. 53.
7. Details on the four dimensions of food insecurity can be found in Annex 2 of FAO (2015), ibid., p. 48. For more on the GHI, see von Grebmer, Klaus, Saltzman, Amy, Birol, Ekin, Weismann,

Doris, Prasai, Nilam, Yin, Sandra, Yohannes, Yisehac, and
Menon, Purnima (2014), *Global Hunger Index: The Challenge
of Hidden Hunger*, Washington, DC: International Food Policy
Research Institute, October.
   This discussion of world hunger and food security does
not address the important critiques from a food sovereignty
perspective, which emphasizes "the right of peoples to healthy
and culturally appropriate food produced through ecologically
sound and sustainable methods, and their right to define their
own food and agriculture systems," viacampesina.org/en/index.
php/organisation-mainmenu-44. Food sovereignty has been
championed by Via Campesina, among other groups. See their
website at viacampesina.org.

8. Davis, Mike (2002), *Late Victorian Holocausts: El Niño Famines
   and the Making of the Third World*, London: Verso Books, pp. 9
   and 11. As grain reserves were exported and sold on the world
   market, instances of famine or food insecurity became more
   likely. This is reminiscent of the dynamics of the global food
   crisis in 1972, which was partly triggered by the US selling
   most of its grain reserves to the Soviet Union. See Morgan,
   Merchants of Grain, op. cit.; and Winders, "The Food Crisis and
   the Deregulation of Agriculture," op. cit.
9. Davis, *Late Victorian Holocausts*, op. cit., p. 315.
10. Ibid., p. 318.
11. Statistics on British wheat imports come from Mitchell, *British
   Historical Statistics*, op. cit., p. 224. These statistics appear in
   Mitchell's book as hundredweight (cwt), and they have been
   converted into million metric tons here.
12. Polanyi, *The Great Transformation*, op. cit., p. 160.
13. Davis, *Late Victorian Holocausts*, op. cit., p. 312.
14. Kugelman, Michael (2010), "Pakistan's Food Insecurity: Roots,
   Ramifications, and Responses," pp. 5–30 in *Hunger Pains:
   Pakistan's Food Insecurity*, edited by Michael Kugelman and
   Robert M. Hathaway, Washington, DC: The Woodrow Wilson
   Center, p. 6.
15. Within a few weeks of the protests, Mexican President
   Felipe Calderón had managed to contain most of the price
   increases by forging an agreement between the government
   and the corn and tortilla industry that worked to cap prices. A
   few years later, observers believed that the spike in tortilla prices

resulted largely from hoarding by large corn flour companies
holding back supplies to take advantage of rising grain prices in
the world economy. See Keleman, Alder, and Rano, Hugo Garcia
(2011), "The Mexican Tortilla Crisis of 2007: The Impacts of
Grain-Price Increases on Food-Production Chains," *Development
in Practice* 21(4–5): 550–65. Importantly, some observers have
noted that these protests – like so many collective actions – were
not entirely spontaneous mass reactions to price increases.
Instead, these "tortilla riots" were coordinated protests grounded
in Mexican politics. For example, see Laudan, Rachel (2008),
"The January 2007 'Tortilla Riots' in Mexico. Really?" available
at http://www.rachellaudan.com/2008/07/the-january-2007-
tortilla-riots-in-mexico-really.html.

16. Several sources discuss the political instability during the global
food crisis: Bello, *The Food Wars*, op. cit.; Holt-Gimenez and
Patel, *Food Rebellions!*, op. cit.; Bush, Ray (2010), "Food Riots:
Poverty, Power, and Protest," *Journal of Agrarian Change* 10(1):
119–29; and Schneider, " 'We are Hungry!' " op. cit.

17. Again, disagreement exists over trends in world hunger, in part
because the FAO recently revised its method for measuring
world hunger. This revision lowered its estimate of world
hunger. In fact, Frances Moore Lappe and her colleagues
show that this change in measurement largely reversed the
trends in hunger during the 2000s. The newer measure of
"prevalence of undernourishment" shows the rate of world
hunger declining, but the previous FAO measure of world
hunger showed the rate increasing during the 2000s. See
Lappe, et al., "How We Count Hunger Matters," op. cit.,
p. 252. Regardless, there is agreement on the effects of recent
events. For example, Bryan McDonald notes, "While chronic
hunger has been an issue of global concern for decades, recent
events, including a global recession and rising food prices,
have significantly increased the number of chronically hungry
people." McDonald, Bryan L. (2010), *Food Security*, Cambridge:
Polity Press, p. 4.

18. Initial explanations of the 2008 global food crisis tended to
focus on the supply of and demand for grains as well as several
other factors: oil prices, biofuels policies, export restrictions,
and financial markets. For discussions of these factors, see
Bello, *The Food Wars*, op. cit.; Clapp, Jennifer (2012), *Food,*

Cambridge: Polity Press, especially ch. 5; and Winders, "The Food Crisis and the Deregulation of Agriculture, " op. cit.

Regarding the argument that food crises are caused by inadequate production, Amartya Sen notes, "some of the worst famines have taken place with no significant decline in food availability per head." As examples of such instances, Sen points to the Bengal famine of 1943, the Ethiopian famine of 1972–4, and the Bangladesh famine of 1974. Of course, one might look at these famines from a global, or world-economic, perspective and focus on the shared timing of what appear to be largely localized famines in the early 1940s and 1972–4. Such shared connections and world-economic dynamics are, in part, the focus of this book. Sen, Amartya (1981), *Poverty and Famines: An Essay on Entitlement and Deprivation*, Oxford: Oxford University Press, p. 7.

19. Timmer, C. Peter, and Dawe, David (2010), "Food Crises Past, Present (and Future?): Will We Ever Learn," pp. 3–11 in *The Rice Crisis: Markets, Policies, and Food Security*, edited by David Dawe, London: Earthscan and FAO, p. 7. Dawe and Slayton state, "India's decision to restrict rice exports had its roots in weather-related damage to its 2006 wheat crop. . . . As a result, India bartered rice for wheat by reducing both wheat imports and rice exports. This stabilized aggregate national cereal supplies and eliminated the need for wheat imports." Dawe, David, and Slayton, Tom (2010), "The World Rice Market Crisis of 2007–2008," pp. 15–28 in *The Rice Crisis*, op. cit., p. 19.

20. Borras, Santurnino M., Jr, McMichael, Philip, and Scoones, Ian (2010), "The Politics of Biofuels, Land, and Agrarian Change," *Journal of Peasant Studies* 37(4): 575–92, p. 577.

21. Bello, *The Food Wars*, op. cit., ch. 6; Baines, "Fuel, Feed and the Corporate Restructuring of the Food Regime," op. cit.

22. Clapp, *Food*, op. cit., p. 143.

23. Timmer and Dawe, "Food Crises," op. cit. p. 7. For more on the financialization of agriculture see Clapp, *Food*, op. cit., ch. 5; Clapp, Jennifer, and Helleiner, Eric (2012), "Troubled Futures? The Global Food Crisis and the Politics of Agricultural Derivatives Regulation," *Review of International Political Economy* 19(2): 181–207; Martin, Sarah J., and Clapp, Jennifer (2015), "Finance for Agriculture or Agriculture for Finance," *Journal of Agrarian Change* 15(4): 549–59; and Fuchs, Doris, Meyer-Eppler, Richard, and Hamenstadt, Ulrich (2013), "Food

for Thought: The Politics of Financialization in the Agrifood System," *Competition and Change* 17(3): 219–33.

24. Jenkins, J. Craig, and Scanlan, Steven (2001), "Food Security in Less Developed Countries, 1970 to 1990," *American Sociological Review* 66(5): 718–44, p. 718.

25. Rosen, Stacey, Meade, Brigit, Shapouri, Shahla, D'Souza, Anna, and Rada, Nicholas (2012), "International Food Security Assessment, 2012–2022," Economic Research Service, USDA, GFA-23, July 2012.

26. Austin, Kelly F., McKinney, Laura, and Thompson, Gretchen (2012), "Agricultural Trade Dependency and the Threat of Starvation: A Cross-National Analysis of Hunger as Unequal Exchange," *International Journal of Sociology* 42(2): 66–90, p. 86.

27. In 2011, food security in India and Pakistan was categorized "Alarming," which is the second worst rating in the GHI, behind "Extremely Alarming." Most countries in these two categories are in Africa or Asia. By 2014, both countries had shown improvement in food security and moved to the category of "Serious." von Grebmer, et al., *Global Hunger Index*, op. cit., pp. 18–19.

28. Toor, Saadia (2010), "Structural Dimensions of Food Insecurity in Pakistan," pp. 99–115 in *Hunger Pains: Pakistan's Food Insecurity*, edited by Michael Kugelman and Robert M. Hathaway, Washington, DC: The Woodrow Wilson Center, p. 100.

29. Readers can find more about quinoa in several sources: Romero, Simon, and Shahriari, Sara (2011), "Quinoa's Global Success Creates Quandary at Home," *New York Times*, March 19; Hamilton, Lisa H. (2014), "The Quinoa Quarrel: Who Owns the World's Greatest Superfood?" *Harper's Magazine*, May: 35–42; and Hellin, Jon, and Higman, Sophie (2005), "Crop Diversity and Livelihood Security in the Andes," *Development in Practice* 15(2): 165–74.

30. The beef industry in India asserts that its beef comes from buffalo not cows, which are considered sacred in India and are protected by laws that prevent their slaughter and the export of beef. Gopal, Sena Desai (2015), "Selling the Sacred Cow: India's Contentious Beef Industry," *The Atlantic*, February.

31. Institution of Mechanical Engineers (2013), "Global Food: Waste Not, Want," London, p. 12.

32. Bush, "Food Riots," op. cit., p. 120.

5 GENETICALLY ENGINEERED GRAINS

1. For details about the crisis involving StarLink maize, see Taylor,
   Michael R., and Tick, Jody S. (2001), *The StarLink Case: Issues
   for the Future*, Pew Initiative on Food and Biotechnology. See
   also Schurman, Rachel, and Munro, William A. (2010), *Fighting
   for the Future of Food: Activists Versus Agribusiness in the Struggle
   Over Biotechnology*, Minneapolis: University of Minnesota
   Press; and Clapp, Jennifer (2008), "Illegal GMO Releases and
   Corporate Responsibility: Questioning the Effectiveness of
   Voluntary Measures," *Ecological Economics* 66: 348–58.
2. Schurman, and Munro, *Fighting for the Future of Food*, op. cit.,
   p. 136. The farmers sued because of the decline in US corn prices
   due to the crisis caused by StarLink corn entering the food system.
3. Both quotations in this paragraph come from Kinchy, Abby
   (2012), *Seeds, Science, and Struggle: The Global Politics of
   Transgenic Crops*, Cambridge, MA: The MIT Press, p. 6.
4. Fernandez-Cornejo, Jorge, Weschler, Seth, Livingston, Michael,
   and Mitchell, Lorraine (2014), *Genetically Engineered Crops in
   the United States*, Economic Research Service, USDA, Number
   162, p. 1. They also state that "Several second-generation GE
   crops have been approved by APHIS: high-lysine corn, reduced-
   nicotine tobacco, high-oleic acid soybean oil, stearidonic acid-
   producing soybeans, improved fatty acid-profile soybeans,
   altered-flower color roses (blue), oil profile-altered canola, and
   alpha amylase corn. Overall, nearly 20 percent of the approvals
   for deregulation (as of September 2013) are second-generation
   crops," ibid., p. 1, note 3.
5. In 1996, these GE tomatoes were introduced in the
   United Kingdom as an ingredient in tomato paste marketed
   by Zeneca and sold in Safeway and Sainsbury's grocery stores.
   Initially, the Zeneca tomato paste with GE tomatoes sold well,
   and consumers bought more than 1 million cans of the paste.
   Sales began to decline in 1998 after a report that laboratory tests
   with rats showed that the GE tomato paste caused biological
   changes. The report was later determined to be incorrect, but
   the Zeneca tomato paste did not make a recovery in the market
   and was pulled. So, in contrast to the experience of the GE
   tomato in the US, consumer reaction in the EU – after more
   than a year – played a central role in the product's commercial

demise. For the Flavr Savr tomato story, see Charles, Dan (2002), *Lords of the Harvest: Biotech, Big Money, and the Future of Food*, New York: Basic Books, ch. 10. See also Bruening, G., and Lyons, J.M. (2000), "The Case of the Flavr Savr Tomato," *California Agriculture* 54(4): 6–7.

6. For the US, see Kloppenburg, Jack Ralph, Jr. (2004), *First the Seed: The Political Economy of Plant Biotechnology* (2nd edn.), Madison: University of Wisconsin Press, p. 296. For global production, see Kinchy, *Seeds, Science, and Struggle*, op. cit., p. 6.

7. Statistics for 1996 come for the Economic Research Service (ERS) of the USDA, "Adoption of Genetically Engineered Crops in the U.S.: Recent Trends in GE Adoption," available at http://www.ers.usda.gov/data-products/adoption-of-genetically-engineered-crops-in-the-us/recent-trends-in-ge-adoption.aspx. Statistics for 2015 come from the National Agricultural Statistics Service (NASS) of the USDA, "Acreage," June 2015, available at http://usda.mannlib.cornell.edu/usda/nass/Acre/2010s/2015/Acre-06-30-2015.pdf. See also acreage estimates in Fernandez-Cornejo, et al., *Genetically Engineered Crops*, op. cit., table 3, p. 9.

8. James, Clive (2014), *Global Status of Commercialized Biotech/GM Crops: 2014 (Executive Summary)*, International Service for the Acquisition of Agri-Biotech Applications (ISAAA), Brief 49, available at http://www.isaaa.org/resources/publications/briefs/49/.

9. Ibid., p. 11.

10. Ibid., pp. 10–11.

11. Howard, Philip H. (2009), "Visualizing Consolidation in the Seed Industry," *Sustainability* 1: 1266–87. Howard, *Concentration and Power in the Food System*, op. cit., pp. 110–11. Kinchy, *Seeds, Science, and Struggle*, op. cit. For the share of the seed market in 2009, see ETC Group (2011), *Who Will Control the Green Economy?*, p. 22, available at http://www.etcgroup.org/content/who-will-control-green-economy-0.

12. Howard, "Visualizing Consolidation," op. cit., see pp. 1273, 1276, and figure 2.

13. Falkner, Robert (2009), *Business Power and Conflict in International Environmental Politics*, New York: Palgrave Macmillan. Robin, Marie-Monique (2010), *The World According to Monsanto: Pollution, Corruption, and the Control of Our Food*

Supply – An Investigation into the World's Most Controversial Seed Company, New York: New Press.

14. Pechlaner, Gabriela (2012), *Corporate Crops: Biotechnology, Agriculture, and the Struggle for Control*, Austin: University of Texas Press. See also Kloppenburg, *First the Seed*, op. cit.

15. For adoption rates of GE crops in the US, see note 7. For GE canola in Canada, see James, *Global Status of Commercialized Biotech: 2014*, op. cit. And for statistics for Argentina and Brazil, see James, Clive (2012), *Global Status of Commercialized Biotech/ GM Crops: 2012*, International Service for the Acquisition of Agri-Biotech Applications (ISAAA), Brief 44.

16. Klumper, Wilhelm, and Qaim, Matin (2014), "A Meta-Analysis of the Impacts of Genetically Modified Crops," *PLOS One* 9(11): 1–7.

17. Jussaume, Raymond, Kondoh, Kazumi, and Ostrom, Marcy (2004), "An Investigation into the Potential Introduction of Roundup-Ready Wheat," Paper presented at the Annual Meeting of the International Rural Sociology Association.

18. In addition to StarLink being a potential allergen, Bt10 maize offers another example of potential health risks. Bt10 maize, developed by Syngenta in the early 2000s, "contains an antibiotic resistant marker gene, which raised concerns about its health impacts, as it was feared that widespread release of the variety could result in the transfer of resistance to the commonly used antibiotic, ampicillin." Bt10 maize was not approved for commercial planting in any country, but it nonetheless made its way into the global food system in 2004. Clapp, "Illegal GMO Releases and Corporate Responsibility," op. cit., p. 353.

19. Eaton, Emily (2013), *Growing Resistance: Canadian Farmers and the Politics of Genetically Modified Wheat*, Winnipeg: University of Manitoba Press.

20. This, of course, happens with conventional seeds and herbicides. The pace of resistance has the potential to be faster with GE crops as they allow farmers to rely on a single herbicide rather than a more comprehensive weed management system, which is often found in conventional farming.

21. Bunge, Jacob (2015), "EPA Urges Limits on GMO Corn; Bug Adapts," *Wall Street Journal*, March 6: B1, B2.

22. Eaton, *Growing Resistance*, op. cit., p. 103.

23. The Pew survey is cited in Paarlberg, Robert (2008), *Starved*

for Science: How Biotechnology is Being Kept Out of Africa,
Cambridge, MA: Harvard University Press, p. 22.

24. Ibid., especially Chapter 1.
25. See the "EU Register of authorized GM Products" on the
European Commission website at http://ec.europa.eu/food/
dyna/gm_register/index_en.cfm. See also Nelsen, Arthur
(2015), "EU Clears Path for 17 New GM Foods," *The Guardian*,
April 16; Smith, Jeremy (2008), "EU Approves Genetically
Modified Soybean for Import," Reuters December 4; and
Mitchell, Peter (2007), "Europe's Anti-GMO Stance to Presage a
Feed Shortage?," *Nature Biotechnology* 25: 1065–6.
26. On the CWB and its survey, see Pechlaner, *Corporate Crops*, op.
cit., p. 106. For the quote, see Magnan, Andre (2007), "Strange
Bedfellows: Contentious Coalitions and the Politics of GM
Wheat," *Canadian Review of Sociology and Anthropology* 44(3):
289–317, p. 310.
27. Heller, Chaia (2006), "Post-Industrial 'Quality Agricultural
Discourse': Techniques of Governance and Resistance in the
French Debate Over GM Crops," *Social Anthropology* 14(3): 319–34.
28. Bunge, Jacob (2014), "Cargill Sues Syngenta Over Sale of GMO
Seeds Unapproved in China," *Wall Street Journal*, September
24; Bunge, Jacob (2014), "ADM Sues Syngenta Over Genetically
Engineered Corn," *Wall Street Journal*, November 19; Bunge,
Jacob (2014), "Syngenta Sues Grain-Trading Firms in Corn
Dispute," *Wall Street Journal*, November 20.
29. Falkner, *Business Power and Conflict*, op. cit., pp. 144–5.
30. Paarlberg, Robert (2001), *The Politics of Precaution: Genetically
Modified Crops in Developing Countries*, Baltimore: Johns
Hopkins University Press, p. 14.
31. This quotation about Syngenta is taken from the Golden Rice
Project website: http://www.goldenrice.org/, accessed February
8, 2016.
32. The quotation on the protest comes from Harmon, Amy (2013),
"Golden Rice: Lifesaver?" *New York Times*, August 25.
33. On the Bt corn protest and adoption by farmers see, Cabanilla,
Liborio S. (2007), "Socio-Economic and Political Concerns for
GM Foods and Biotechnology Adoption in the Philippines,"
AgBioForum 10(3): 178–83.
34. Gunther, Marc (2007), "Attack of the Mutant Rice," *Fortune*
156(1): 74–80.

35. Clapp, "Illegal GMO Releases," op. cit., p. 354.
36. Grasso, June (2011), "Bayer Pays $750 Million to Settle Rice Contamination Cases," *Business Wire*, July 1.
37. Clapp, "Illegal GMO Releases," op. cit.; Clapp, *Food*, op. cit.; Sell, Susan K. (2009), "Corporations, Seeds, and Intellectual Property Rights Governance," pp. 187–223 in *Corporate Power in Global Agrifood Governance*, op. cit.
38. Magnan, "Strange Bedfellows," op. cit., p. 306.

6 SEEDS OF CHANGE

1. This statement comes from La Via Campesina's website, www. viacampesina.org.
2. Borras, Saturnino M., Jr. (2008), "La Vía Campesina and its Global Campaign for Agrarian Reform," *Journal of Agrarian Change* 8(2–3): 258–89.
3. Hall, Derek (2013), *Land*, Cambridge: Polity Press, p. 141. While my focus in this chapter is resistance to changes in land tenure and property relations, Hall rightly points out that "some rural people have been willing to see their land acquired by states or businesses, to welcome expanded government authority over their lives and to adapt to new regulations around titling and conservation if they see some benefit for themselves. People may seek to engage with these processes on their own terms, and we cannot assume 'resistance' as the natural response," p. 145.
4. Ibid., p. 141.
5. Karl Polanyi made three important points about land in this regard. First, he argued that land was a "fictitious commodity" because it cannot be produced for the sole purpose of selling on the market – it is simply nature, and it exists regardless of the market economy. Second, land is so essential to human existence and our communities that it is particularly vulnerable to the vagaries of the market (e.g., sharp declines in prices, exploitation for profits), and this can lead to significant threats to the well-being of communities and people. Third and finally, Polanyi discussed the process of commodifying land and of protecting land from the market as part of the double movement of the market economy, in which some forces advocate greater reliance on market processes (e.g., prices) while other forces

push for protections from the market (e.g., through regulations). Polanyi also emphasized the role of the state in both sides of this double movement toward the market and toward regulation. See Polanyi, *The Great Transformation*, op. cit.

6. Karl Marx referred to the process of accumulation through dispossession as "primitive accumulation," which he saw as the initial stage in the creation of the market economy. Marx, Karl (1990), *Capital: A Critique of Political Economy, Volume I*, New York: Penguin.

7. Barry, Tom (1995), *Zapata's Revenge: Free Trade and the Farm Crisis in Mexico*, Boston: South End Press.

8. Friedmann, and McMichael, "Agriculture and the State System," op. cit.

9. Barry, *Zapata's Revenge*, op. cit., p. 23.

10. Lie, John (2000), *Han Unbound: The Political Economy of South Korea*, Stanford, CA: Stanford University Press, pp. 11–12.

11. Ibid. See also Linklater, Andro (2013), *Owning the Earth: The Transforming History of Land Ownership*, New York: Bloomsbury.

12. Araghi, Farshad (1995), "Global Depeasantization, 1945–1990," *The Sociological Quarterly* 36(2): 337–68, p. 346.

13. On land reform in Thailand see Ramsay, James Ansil (1982), "The Limits of Land Reform in Thailand," *Journal of Developing Areas* 16(2): 173–96.

14. Lahiff, Edward (2007), " 'Willing Buyer, Willing Seller': South Africa's Failed Experiment in Market-Led Agrarian Reform," *Third World Quarterly* 28(8): 1577–97, p. 1581.

15. Ibid., p. 1585.

16. World Bank (2008), "Accelerating Inclusive Growth and Deepening Fiscal Stability Draft Report for the Philippines Development Forum 2008," p. 82. Draft report available at http://siteresources.worldbank.org/INTPHILIPPINES/Resources/WBReport-PDF2008.pdf. On Brazil, see Wolford, Wendy (2007), "Land Reform in the Time of Neoliberalism: A Many-Splendored Thing," *Antipode* 39(3): 550–70. On the Philippines, see Bello, *The Food Wars*, op. cit. Borras, Saturnino M., Jr., Carranza, Danilo, and Franco, Jennifer C. (2007), "Anti-Poverty or Anti-Poor?: The World Bank's Market-Led Agrarian Reform Experiment in the Philippines," *Third World Quarterly* 28(8): 1557–76.

17. Barry, *Zapata's Revenge*, op. cit., p. 177.

18. Chuang, Julia (2015), "Urbanization through Dispossession:

Survival and Stratification in China's New Townships," *Journal of Peasant Studies* 42(2): 275–94; Yardley, Jim (2004), "A Chinese History of Dispossession and Exploitation," *New York Times*, December 8; Harvey, David (2003), *The New Imperialism*, Oxford: Oxford University Press.

19. The examples of land grabs come from the land grab database published by GRAIN and available at www.grain.org. See also Hall, *Land*, op. cit.; Fairbairn, Madeleine (2014), " 'Like Gold With Yield': Evolving Intersections between Farmland and Finance," *Journal of Peasant Studies* 41(5): 777–95; McMichael, Philip (2012), "The Land Grab and Corporate Food Regime Restructuring," *Journal of Peasant Studies* 39(3–4): 681–701; and Clapp, *Food*, op. cit., pp. 147–55. There is now a large and growing literature on land grabs. See the Selected Readings at the end of this book for more sources.

20. Winders, "The Vanishing Free Market, " op. cit.

21. Winders, *The Politics of Food Supply*, op. cit.

22. Steinfeld, Henning, Gerber, Pierre, Wassenaar, Tom, Castell, Vincent, Rosales, Mauricio, and de Haan, Cees (2006), "Livestock's Long Shadow: Environmental Issues and Options," Report for the Food and Agriculture Organization of the United Nations. See also Weis, *The Ecological Hoofprint*, op. cit. More recently, the United Nations has encouraged a global reduction in meat consumption and a shift toward a more vegan diet. See Carus, Felicity (2010), "UN Urges Global Move to Meat and Dairy-Free Diet," *The Guardian*, June 2, available at http://www.theguardian.com/environment/2010/jun/02/un-report-meat-free-diet.

23. The quotation from Via Campesina is quoted in Fitting, Elizabeth (2011), *The Struggle for Maize: Campesinos, Workers, and Transgenic Corn in the Mexican Countryside*, Durham, NC: Duke University Press, p. 111.

24. McMichael, "The Land Grab," op. cit., p. 682. On the connection between agriculture and international migration, see Barry, *Zapata's Revenge*, op. cit.; Jaffee, Daniel (2007), *Brewing Justice: Fair Trade Coffee, Sustainability, and Survival*, Berkeley: University of California Press; and Schwartzman, Kathleen C. (2013), *The Chicken Trail: Following Workers, Migrants, and Corporations across the Americas*, Ithaca, NY: Cornell University Press.

Selected Readings

Readers interested in the issues raised in this book can find further reading in a number of books and journals. There are several books and many scholarly articles about the political economy and geopolitics of maize, rice, and wheat, as well as other grains. The endnotes, of course, list many such sources that I relied on for this book. But there are more still.

Chapter 1 begins with the ubiquity of grains in our national and global food systems. Several books highlight this omnipresence of grains, the most noteworthy, perhaps is Michael Pollan's *The Omnivore's Dilemma: A Natural History of Four Meals* (New York: Penguin Press, 2006). Part I, which includes the first seven chapters of Pollan's book examines how pervasive maize is in contemporary diets, especially in the US. Andre Magnan, *When Wheat Was King: The Rise and Fall of the Canada–UK Grain Trade* (Vancouver: University of British Columbia Press, 2016) focuses on Canada and Great Britain in the global wheat trade. Dan Morgan's *Merchants of Grain* (New York: Penguin Books, 1979) provides a look at the long history of the grain trade, particularly wheat. With a focus on California, see Richard A. Walker, *The Conquest of Bread: 150 Years of Agribusiness in California* (New York: The New Press, 2004). For readers interested in maize in particular, a good introduction can be found in Arturo Warman's *Corn and Capitalism: How a Botanical Bastard Grew to Global Dominance* (Chapel Hill: University of North Carolina Press, 2003). And A.J.H. Latham provides a short introduction to the world of rice in *Rice: The Primary Commodity* (New York: Routledge, 1998). Francesca Bray's *The Rice Economies: Technology and Development in Asian Societies* (New York: Basil Blackwell, 1989) is a classic and comprehensive look at the social and political context of rice cultivation.

This first chapter also examines the contours of the global food system, and readers can find more discussion of this in several books. Two books provide a particularly nice introduction to the global food system: Tony Weis, *The Global Food Economy: The Battle for the Future of Farming* (London: Zed Books, 2007) and Raj Patel, *Stuffed and Starved: The Hidden Battle for the World Food System* (New York: Melville House, 2012). Jennifer Clapp's *Food* (Cambridge: Polity Press, 2012) also provides an excellent overview of the global food system. For a look at recent trends in market concentration in the food system, see Philip H. Howard's *Concentration and Power in the Food System: Who Controls What We Eat?* (New York: Bloomsbury Academic, 2016). Robert Paarlberg explores a variety of dimensions of the food system in *Food Politics: What Everyone Needs to Know* (New York: Oxford University Press, 2010). Looking at one particular sector of the global food system, Elizabeth R. DeSombre and J. Samuel Barkin's *Fish* (Cambridge: Polity Press, 2011) shows how some governments attempt to regulate fishing to make it more sustainable while others use the industry as a means of economic development, and the global implications of such efforts.

Chapter 1 also examines the dynamics of political and economic divisions within agriculture, highlighting the potential splits between food grains and feed grains. A good introduction to the development and impact of the global meat industry can be found in Tony Weis's *The Ecological Hoofprint: The Global Burdens of Industrial Livestock* (New York: Zed Books, 2013). See also Joseph Baines, "Fuel, Feed and the Corporate Restructuring of the Food Regime," *Journal of Peasant Studies*

2015, 42(2): 295–321, which explores political and economic divisions between feed grains and biofuels, what Baines calls the "Animal Processor nexus" and the "Agro-Trader nexus," respectively. Baines argues that the rise in maize prices associated with the ethanol boom in the US increased the earnings of the Agro-Trader nexus and corn growers but reduced earnings for the Animal Processor nexus and livestock farmers.

Finally, Chapter 1 also highlights the influence of agrifood corporations, and there are several sources that offer more details on this issue. For an informative examination of the primary corporate actors in grains, especially the grain trade, see Sophia Murphy, David Burch, and Jennifer Clapp, *Secrets: The World's Largest Grain Traders and Global Agriculture* (Oxford: Oxfam Research Reports, 2012). See also Jennifer Clapp, "ABCD and Beyond: From Grain Merchants to Agricultural Value Chain Managers," *Canadian Food Studies* 2015, 32(2): 126–35. Jennifer Clapp and Doris Fuchs's edited *Corporate Power in Global Agrifood Governance* (Cambridge, MA: The MIT Press, 2009) offers a series of essays that examine the influence of agrifood corporations on the global food system. The chapters in this book show how corporations have influenced the construction of international rules that govern food, and several chapters focus on biotechnology. Readers can find an accessible discussion of the role of finance in the food sector in Kara Newman, *The Secret Financial Life of Food: From Commodities Markets to Supermarkets* (New York: Columbia University Press, 2013), as well as *Hungry Capital: The Financialization of Food* (Winchester: Zero Books, 2013) by Luigi Russi. For more on political and economic divisions and conflicts between corporations, see Robert Falkner, *Business Power and Conflict in International Environmental Politics* (New York: Palgrave Macmillan, 2008). Readers interested in how the market economy can contribute to such divisions and conflicts might look at Karl Polanyi, *The Great*

Transformation: The Political and Economic Origins of Our Time (Boston: Beacon Press, 1944/2001), which is a classic essay on the conflicts and contradictions that can result from market processes, such as commodification. For a related and sophisticated analysis of how social and historical context shapes the economic interests of different segments of capital, see Peter A. Swenson, *Capitalists Against Markets: The Making of Labor Markets and Welfare States in the United States and Sweden* (New York: Oxford University Press, 2002).

Chapter 2 concentrates on the global food system for most of the twentieth century, up to about 1975. *The Politics of Food Supply: U.S. Agricultural Policy in the World Economy* (New Haven, CT: Yale University Press, 2009) by Bill Winders highlights how divisions in agriculture – particularly between cotton, maize, and wheat – shaped US agricultural policy throughout the twentieth century. Ann-Christina L. Knudsen examines European agricultural policy, particularly the formation of the CAP, in *Farmers on Welfare: The Making of Europe's Common Agricultural Policy* (Ithaca, NY: Cornell University Press, 2009). A nice comparison of the development and retrenchment of agricultural policy can be found in Adam Sheingate's *The Rise of the Agricultural Welfare State: Institutions and Interest Group Power in the United States, France, and Japan* (Princeton, NJ: Princeton University Press, 2001). Sheingate emphasizes how politics and the shape of political institutions shaped the formation, development, and ultimate decline of supply management policy in these three countries. Nadine Lehrer's *U.S. Farm Bills and Policy Reforms: Ideological Conflicts Over World Trade, Renewable Energy, and Sustainable Agriculture* (New York: Cambria Press, 2010) examines the influence of environmentalism in recent US farm bills. Kym Anderson and Yujiro Hayami's edited book, *The Political Economy of Agricultural Protection: East Asia in International Perspective* (Boston: Allen & Unwin, 1986), offers a look at the development and details of agricultural protectionism and supply management policy in several Asian countries, including South Korea and Japan. And Kym Anderson's *The Political Economy of Agricultural Price Distortions* (Cambridge: Cambridge University Press, 2010) offers a view of supply management policy from an economics standpoint. For a global perspective on agricultural policy, see also E. Wesley F. Peterson, *A Billion Dollars a Day: The Economics and Politics of Agricultural Subsidies* (Oxford: Wiley-Blackwell, 2009). For a discussion of policy issues facing poorer countries, readers might turn to Per Pinstrup-Anderson and Derrill D. Watson II, *Food Policy for Developing Countries: The Role of Government in Global, National, and Local Food Systems* (Ithaca, NY: Cornell University Press, 2011). On GATT and WTO negotiations, see Jennifer Clapp, "WTO Agriculture Negotiations: Implications for the Global South," *Third World Quarterly* 2006, 27(4): 563–77.

On the different bases of the British and US food regimes, see Harriet Friedmann and Philip McMichael, "Agriculture and the State System: The Rise and Decline of National Agricultures, 1870 to the Present," *Sociologia Ruralis* 1989, 29(2): 93–117; and Bill Winders, "The Vanishing Free Market: The Formation and Spread of the British and US Food Regimes," *Journal of Agrarian Change* 2009, 9(3): 315–44. For more on international trade flows in the late nineteenth and early twentieth centuries, see Steve C. Topik and Allen Wells, *Global Markets Transformed, 1870–1945* (Cambridge, MA: Belknap Press of Harvard University Press, 2012). Topik and Wells show the rough transition between the British and US food regimes, though they do not use that terminology.

Chapter 3 picks up in 1975 and examines the fundamental shift in the international food regime with the spread of more market-oriented national and international policies. On liberalization in general, see two books by David Harvey:

The New Imperialism (New York: Oxford University Press, 2003) and A Brief History of Neoliberalism (Oxford: Oxford University Press, 2007). See also Immanuel Wallerstein's The Decline of American Power: The U.S. in a Chaotic World (New York: The New Press, 2003), and Globalization and its Discontents (New York: Norton, 2002) by Joseph E. Stiglitz. For a longer view with a focus on the role of finance, see Giovanni Arrighi's The Long Twentieth Century: Money, Power and the Origins of Our Times (London: Verso Books, 2010). Rawi Abdelal examines the rise of global financial markets in the twentieth century in Capital Rules: The Construction of Global Finance (Cambridge, MA: Harvard University Press, 2007). In Business Power in Global Governance (Boulder, CO: Lynne Rienner, 2007), Doris Fuchs examines the influence of transnational corporations in the establishment of new rules of governance in the world economy from the 1980s through the early 2000s. For liberalization in national agricultural policies, see Winders' The Politics of Food Supply and Sheingate's Rise of the Agricultural Welfare State, both already mentioned in the section on Chapter 2. See also Christina L. Davis, Food Fights over Free Trade: How International Institutions Promote Agricultural Trade Liberalization (Princeton, NJ: Princeton University Press, 2005). And on the liberalization of the food regime, see Philip McMichael, Food Regimes and Agrarian Questions (Halifax, NS: Fernwood Books, 2013).

For a look at how this shift has resulted in greater instability for agriculture in the world economy, particularly in terms of prices, see Bill Winders, Alison Heslin, Gloria Ross, Hannah Weksler, and Seanna Berry, "Life After the Regime: Market Instability and the Fall of the U.S. Food Regime," Agriculture and Human Values 2016, 33(1): 73–88. On Mexico, see Tom Barry's Zapata's Revenge: Free Trade and the Farm Crisis in Mexico (Boston: South End Press, 1995). The effect that liberalization in the world economy has had on workers and migration can be seen very clearly in Kathleen C. Schwartzman's *The Chicken Trail: Following Workers, Migrants, and Corporations across the Americas* (Ithaca, NY: Cornell University Press, 2013). Amy Quark examines how the US food regime and consequent liberalization of the world economy influenced world cotton production and trade in her book, *Global Rivalries: Standards Wars and the Transnational Cotton Trade* (Chicago: University of Chicago Press, 2013).

For more on the expanding meat industry and its consequences, see Tony Weis, *The Ecological Hoofprint*, already mentioned. See also Erik Marcus, *Meat Market: Animals, Ethics, and Money* (Boston: Brio Press, 2005); David A. Nibert, *Animal Oppression and Human Violence: Domesecration, Capitalism, and Global Conflict* (New York: Columbia University Press, 2013); Timothy Pachirat, *Every Twelve Seconds: Industrialized Slaughter and the Politics of Sight* (New Haven, CT: Yale University Press, 2011); Daniel Imhoff (ed.), *The CAFO Reader: The Tragedy of Industrial Animal Factories* (Los Angeles: Watershed Media, 2010); and David Kirby, *Animal Factory: The Looming Threat of Industrial Pig, Dairy, and Poultry Farms to Humans and the Environment* (New York: St. Martin's Press, 2011). For a detailed look at the state of global meat production and its effects, see the 2006 report by the Food and Agriculture Organization (FAO), "Livestock's Long Shadow" (available at www.fao.org).

Chapter 4 focuses on the issues of world hunger and food security. For a good introduction to these issues, see Bryan L. McDonald, *Food Security* (Cambridge: Polity Press, 2010). For a classic view of hunger, see Amartya Sen, *Poverty and Famines: An Essay on Entitlement and Deprivation* (Oxford: Oxford University Press, 1981). Two other books provide basic introductions to the issue of world hunger: Howard Leathers and Phillips Foster, *The World Food Problem: Toward Ending Undernutrition in the Third World* (Boulder, CO: Lynne

Rienner, 2009), and Frances Moore Lappe and Joseph Collins, *World Hunger: 10 Myths* (New York: Grove Press, 2015). See also, Gordon Conway, *One Billion Hungry: Can We Feed the World?* (Ithaca, NY: Cornell University Press, 2012). For a historical look at the construction of our understanding of world hunger and how it fits with the idea of development, see Nick Cullather, *The Hungry World: America's Cold War Battle Against Poverty in Asia* (Cambridge, MA: Harvard University Press, 2010). On the role of markets and colonization in the famines in Asia, Africa, and Latin America in the late 1800s, see Mike Davis, *Late Victorian Holocausts: El Niño Famines and the Making of the Third World* (London: Verso, 2002). John Walton and David Seddon's *Free Markets and Food Riots: The Politics of Global Adjustment* (Cambridge: Blackwell, 1994) shows how austerity measures by the IMF and World Bank from the 1970s to the 1990s contributed to political instability and waves of protests and food riots during those decades.

Several books offer good analyses of the global food crisis of 2008. Jennifer Clapp and Marc J. Cohen's edited volume, *The Global Food Crisis: Governance Challenges and Opportunities* (Waterloo, ON: Wilfrid Laurier University Press, 2009) offers in-depth examinations of the price crisis, the issue of food aid, and attempts at sustainable agriculture as a solution to food crises. *Food Rebellions! Crisis and the Hunger for Justice* (Oxford: Pambazuka Press, 2009) by Eric Holt-Gimenez and Raj Patel looks at how the global food system contributed to the 2008 food crisis. For more on how the liberalization of the world economy contributed to food insecurity and the global food crisis in 2008, see Walden Bello, *The Food Wars* (London: Verso, 2009), as well as *Agriculture and Food in Crisis: Conflict, Resistance, and Renewal* (New York: Monthly Review Press, 2010), edited by Fred Magdoff and Brian Tokar. For more information about the specifics of the rice market and how the food crisis developed regarding rice, see David

Dawe (ed.), *The Rice Crisis: Markets, Policies and Food Security* (London: Earthscan and FAO, 2010). And for a look at how the food crisis affected the Middle East, see Eckart Woertz, *Oil for Food: The Global Food Crisis and the Middle East* (Oxford: Oxford University Press, 2013).

Chapter 5 tackles the issue of biotechnology in agriculture, focusing on the genetic engineering of seeds. There is a substantial literature examining biotechnology in agriculture. Jack Ralph Kloppenburg, Jr. traces the role of technology in seeds and agriculture in *First the Seed: The Political Economy of Plant Biotechnology* (2nd edn.) (Madison: University of Wisconsin Press, 2004). Philip H. Howard examines some of the recent trends in terms of market concentration in biotech agriculture in "Visualizing Consolidation in the Global Seed Industry: 1996–2008," *Sustainability* 2009, 1(4): 1266–87. Dan Charles details the development of biotechnology in agriculture, paying particular attention to the role of various biotech companies, in *Lords of the Harvest: Biotech, Big Money, and the Future of Food* (Cambridge: Basic Books, 2001). See also *Hungry Corporations: Transnational Biotech Companies Colonise the Food Chain* (London: Zed Books, 2003) by Helena Paul and Ricarda Steinbrecher. One book that provides a good introduction on the role and influence of Monsanto is Marie-Monique Robin's *The World According to Monsanto: Pollution, Corruption, and the Control of our Food Supply* (New York: The New Press, 2008).

For more on the struggles against biotechnology in agriculture, see Rachel Schurman and William A. Munro, *Fighting for the Future of Food: Activists Versus Agribusiness in the Struggle Over Biotechnology* (Minneapolis: University of Minnesota Press, 2010). On the response of consumers and efforts to win (GE) labeling requirements and standards, see Carmen Bain and Tamera Dandachi, "Governing GMOs: The (Counter) Movement for Mandatory and Voluntary

Non-GMOs Labels," *Sustainability* 2014, 6(12): 9456–76. For a look at the impact of GE crops in Latin America, see *Food for the Few: Neoliberal Globalism and Biotechnology in Latin America* (Austin: University of Texas Press, 2008), edited by Gerardo Otero. For more positive examinations of biotechnology in agriculture, see two books by Robert Paarlberg: *The Politics of Precaution: Genetically Modified Crops in Developing Countries* (Baltimore: Johns Hopkins University Press, 2001), and *Starved for Science: How Biotechnology is Being Kept Out of Africa* (Cambridge, MA: Harvard University Press, 2008).

For more on GE grains, in particular, there are several books that examine the role of farmers, consumers, corporations, and governments. Gabriela Pechlaner offers an analysis of biotechnology through a comparison of GE cotton in the US, wheat in Canada, and GE canola in Canada in her book, *Corporate Crops: Biotechnology, Agriculture, and the Struggle for Control* (Austin: University of Texas Press, 2012). Emily Eaton examines the politics of GE wheat and canola in Canada in *Growing Resistance: Canadian Farmers and the Politics of Genetically Modified Wheat* (Winnipeg: University of Manitoba Press, 2013). Abby Kinchy compares GE canola in Canada and GE maize in Mexico in her book, *Seeds, Science, and Struggle: The Global Politics of Transgenic Crops* (Cambridge, MA: The MIT Press, 2012). For a detailed looked at GE maize in Mexico, see Elizabeth Fitting, *The Struggle for Maize: Campesinos, Workers, and Transgenic Corn in the Mexican Countryside* (Durham, NC: Duke University Press, 2011). And Chaia Heller examines farmer resistance to GE crops in France, in her book *Food, Farms, and Solidarity: French Farmers Challenge Industrial Agriculture and Genetically Modified Crops* (Durham, NC: Duke University Press, 2012).

Chapter 6 has a central focus on access to land. For a good introduction to land relations, from the idea of property to recent conflicts over land, see Derek Hall's *Land* (Cambridge:

Polity Press, 2013). Recently, "land grabs" have become a visible issue in public discussions. Two books provide particularly good introductions to the process of land grabs: Fred Pearce's *The Land Grabbers: The New Fight Over Who Owns the Earth* (Boston: Beacon Press, 2012), and Michael Kugelman and Susan Levenstein's *The Global Farms Race: Land Grabs, Agricultural Investment, and the Scramble for Food Security* (Washington, DC: Island Press, 2013). Kugelman and Levenstein's book is an edited volume that includes chapters on a variety of dimensions of the land grab phenomenon: the historical roots, environmental implications, and the perspectives of investors, as well as regional perspectives (Asia, Africa, Latin America, Eastern and Central Europe, and Russia). For more on market-led reforms, see *Market-Led Agrarian Reform* (New York: Routledge, 2008), edited by Saturnino M. Borras, Jr., Cristobal Kay, and Edward Lahiff. And for the connection to food regimes, see Philip McMichael, "The 'Land Grab' and Corporate Food Regime Restructuring," *Journal of Peasant Studies* 2012, 39(3/4): 681–701.

Numerous books look at resistance to the expansion of the market economy and its encroachment into peasant and indigenous lands. For an examination of the Via Campesina, see Annette Aurelie Demarais, *La Via Campesina: Globalization and the Power of Peasants* (London: Pluto Press, 2007). The volume edited by Saturnino M. Borras, Jr., Marc Edelman, and Cristobal Kay, *Transnational Agrarian Movements Confronting Globalization* (Oxford: Blackwell, 2008), has chapters that discuss a variety of movements by peasants and indigenous groups. On peasant resistance, in general, see James C. Scott, *Weapons of the Weak: Everyday Forms of Peasant Resistance* (New Haven, CT: Yale University Press, 1989). On the possibility of violence in response to peasant resistance, see Pablo Lapegna, "The Expansion of Transgenic Soybeans and the Killing of Indigenous Peasants in Argentina," *Societies without Borders*

2013, 8(2): 291–308. Lapegna also has a forthcoming book, *Soybeans and Power: Genetically Modified Crops, Environmental Politics, and Social Movements in Argentina* (New York: Oxford University Press).

For readers considering the broader implications of the global food system, the capitalist world economy, and the environment, see Jason W. Moore, *Capitalism in the Web of Life: Ecology and the Accumulation of Capital* (London: Verso Books, 2015). See also Jennifer Clapp and Peter Dauvergne, *Paths to a Green World: The Political Economy of the Global Environment* (Cambridge, MA: The MIT Press, 2005). Another good introduction to some of these issues can be found in Peter Devell's *Globalization and the Environment: Capitalism, Ecology and Power* (Cambridge: Polity Press, 2012). Naomi Klein's *This Changes Everything: Capitalism vs. The Climate* (New York: Simon & Schuster, 2015) examines climate change and touches on agriculture.

Index

Page numbers in *italic* refer to tables

acreage allotments 16
African National Congress
    (ANC) 147
Agreement on Agriculture (AoA)
    62, 70–2
    domestic support 70–1
    export subsidies 71
    market access 71
    resistance to 71–2
Agricultural Adjustment Act
    (1933) 38
agricultural policies
    divisions between 15–18
    see also British food regime;
    liberalization in agriculture;
    supply management
    policies; US food regime
Agricultural Trade Development
    and Assistance Act (1954)
    25
agrifood corporations 5, 8, 19,
    20
    ABCDs 6–7, *7*, 15, 19
    benefits of GE grain
        production 119–20
    competition, new 7
    divisions regarding GE grain
        production 126–8
    political and economic
        influence of 6, 7
    size and geographic reach 7

support for incorporation of
    agriculture into GATT 69
    see also individual corporations
Agrisure Viptera 127, 128
Agro-Trader 78
Al-Khorayef Group 150
Alberta Investment Management
    Company 150
alfalfa 111
Algeria, food riots 6, 89
Aquino, Corazon 148
Arab Spring 6, 81, 89
Archer Daniels Midland (ADM)
    6, 7, 69, 78, 90, 127
Argentina
    Cairns Group member 68–9
    GE grain production 113, 118,
        120, 132, 153
    Grain Regulation Board 39
    maize exports 13, 36
    maize production 13, 36, 118
    soybean exports 13, 132
    soybean production 13, 118, 153
    supply management 37
    wheat exports 45
    wheat production 32, 33
Asgrow Agronomics 116
Australia
    Cairns Group member 68–9
    International Wheat
        Agreement (IWA) 43

Australia (*cont.*)
  price subsidies 39
  supply management policies
    39
  wheat exports 13–14, 45
  wheat production 32, 33–4
Aventis Crop Science 107, 108,
    125, 129

Bacillis thuringiensis (Bt) gene
    107, 111, 113–14, 118, 129
Baines, J. 78
Bangladesh
  food riots 81
  rice production 13
barley
  feed grain 10
  world production of 3, 4
BASF 115
Bayer CropScience 115, 121,
    129–30
biofuels
  contribution to global food
    crisis 91
  expansion in 78–9, 90–1
  maize 12, 78–9, 89, 90
  and shift away from feed/food
    grains production 78, 91
biotech industry
  medicine 115
  mergers and consolidations
    115, 116
  public attitudes to 115–16
  see also genetically engineered
    (GE) grains
Blair House Accord (1992) 70
Bolivia
  food security 98
  quinoa production 99, 100
Bove, Jose 126
Brazil
  biofuel production 90–1
  Cairns Group member 68–9

famines 27
  Fome Zero (Zero Hunger)
    initiative 94
  food security 94
  G23 member 72
  GE grain production 113, 118,
    120, 132, 133, 153
  land reform 145, 148
  maize exports 13, 14–15, 108,
    132, 133
  maize production 13, 14, 36,
    118
  soybean exports 13, 14, 15, 132,
    133
  soybean production 13, 14,
    118, 153
Bretton Woods Accord 55
Britain
  CAP subsidies 67–8
  colonialism 84–8, 105
  Corn Laws 26
  decline of British hegemony
    143
  imperial preferences trading
    system 40–1
  wheat imports 31, 87
  world-economic dominance
    26
British Commonwealth 41
British food regime 22, 140–2,
    151–2
  centrality of wheat 152
  collapse of 31, 143
  and famines 27
  free trade basis 22, 26, 29,
    30–1, 86, 87, 140, 142, 151
  and land expropriation 27
  livestock 151, 152
  market orientation 26
  plantation systems 27
  protectionism 30
  tariffs 30, 31
Bunge 6, 7, 90

Burkina Faso, food riots 81
Burma
    rice exports 34, 46
    stagnating rural economy 35
Bush, R. 105

Cairns Group 68–9, 72, 79, 155
    members 68–9
    targets 69
    and tariff reductions 71
Caldéron, Felipe 168n53
Calgene 110
Cameroon, food riots 81
Canada
    Cairns Group member 68–9
    canola production 120–1, 122,
        125, 133
    GE grain production 113, 118,
        120–1, 122, 125–6, 133
    International Wheat
        Agreement (IWA) 43
    quinoa imports 99
    wheat exports 13–14, 45, 56, 67
    wheat production 32, 33, 34,
        133
Canadian Wheat Board (CWB)
    125
canola 111, 118, 120–1, 122, 125,
    133
Cardenas, Lazaro 143
Cargill 6, 7, 69, 90, 116, 127
Cartagena Protocol on Biosafety
    19, 132
Case–Church Amendment
    (1973) 57
cassava 67
Chiapas rebellion, Mexico 52–3,
    77, 79, 135
child hunger 93
Chile, land reform 145
China
    famines 27
    G23 member 72

and GE grains 114–15, 127–8
incorporation into the world
    economy 86
land reform 149–50
low-wage industrial labor 149,
    150
maize imports 13, 114, 127
maize production 13, 15
rice imports 13
rice production 13
rise of markets in 56
soybean imports 13, 15, 114
soybean production 15
wheat imports 13, 56
wheat production 13
Clapp, J. 7, 130
climate change 158
cocoa 42, 59
Cofco 7
coffee 42, 59
Cold War 76, 144, 145
Colombia
    land reform 145
    per capita maize consumption
        24, 49
    per capita wheat consumption
        24–5, 49
    wheat imports 24, 25, 49
    wheat production 25
colonialism
    British 84–8, 105
    land expropriation 141
    postcolonialism 57
    and rice production 34–5
    "Scramble for Africa" 141
    settler colonies 142
Commodities Futures Trading
    Commission (CFTC) 91
commodity futures market
    91–2
Commodity Futures
    Modernization Act (2000)
    91

commodity investment funds
(CIFs) 91, 92
Common Agricultural Policy
(CAP) 63, 67, 70
communism, decline of 56
impact on markets 76–7
Confederation Paysanne (CP)
126, 136
confined animal feeding
operations (CAFOs) 102,
103, 105
Coolidge, Calvin 38
corn see maize
Corn Laws 26, 30, 31
corn syrup 2, 131
cornmeal 9
Costa Rica, land reform 145
cotton 38, 85, 111, 114
cross-border capital flows
56
cultural role of grains 3
Czech Republic 113

dairy industry 64, 102–3
Davis, M. 84, 85, 86, 87
Dawe, D. 89
Dekalb Genetics 116
differences in grains 8–18
geography of grains 12–15
how grains are used 9–12
national policy differences
15–18
Domínguez, Absalón 52
Dominican Republic, land
reform 145
double movement of the market
22–3
Dow 115
DuPont 20, 78, 115, 116

East Asian Financial crisis (1997)
56
Eaton, E. 121

Ecuador
food security 98
land reform 145
quinoa production 100
Egypt 64
food riots 81
ejidos 53, 143, 144, 149
embedded liberalism 54–5, 56
breakdown of 55, 56, 57, 58
Environmental Protection
Agency (USEPA) 107, 122
Europe
Common Agricultural Policy
(CAP) 63, 67, 70
export subsidies 65–6, 67–8
feed grain imports 63–4
maize production 36
political schisms 67–8
wheat production and exports
63, 64, 64, 65, 65
wheat subsidy war 63–8, 69,
72, 79, 135
see also European Community;
European Union; and
individual nations
European Community (EC)
65–6, 67
European Union (EU)
biofuel production 91
GE grain imports 124–5,
130
GE grain production 113–14,
118, 124
maize imports 124
maize production 13
moratorium on GE crops 132,
133
soybean imports 15, 124
and tariff reductions 71
wheat exports 13–14
wheat production 13
Export Enhancement Program
(EEP) 66

export subsidies 8, 16, 17, 47, 155
  Cairns Group opposition to
    69, 72
  and competitive advantage 17
  and conflicts 17
  function 29
  GATT allowance of 41
  reductions, AoA calls for 71
  surplus grains and 47, 50,
    65–6
  wheat subsidy war 63–8, 69,
    72, 79, 135
  see also under individual nations
export-oriented agriculture
  benefits 94
  contribution to hunger and
    food insecurity 93–7, 157
  restrictions on 90, 92, 94

Falkner, R. 128
famines 20, 27, 84, 86, 87, 105,
    169n56
farmers
  acceptance of GE grain
    production 118–19, 120, 121
  export-oriented farming 14
  mobilization 21, 39, 52–3, 72,
    126, 137
  political and economic
    influence of 6, 136
  resistance to GE grains 125–6,
    133
fast food, grain content of 1
Federal Agriculture
  Improvement and Reform
  Act (1996) 61
feed grains 1, 9, 10, 11–12
  averse to supply management
    policies 17, 18, 50–1, 73
  competitive world markets
    18, 133
  GE feed grains 20, 112, 128,
    131, 134, 135, 157

global demand for 134
  see also under individual grains
financialization of agriculture
    89, 91–2
  commodity futures market
    91–2
First World War 32, 34, 36
fixed currencies 55
Flavr Savr tomatoes 110–11
Fome Zero (Zero Hunger)
    initiative 94
Food and Agricultural
  Organization 10, 59, 81
  food security definition 83
  world hunger estimates 88
  world hunger measures 82
food aid 25, 93
food crises, global 5–6, 57
  see also famines; global food
    crisis (2007–8)
food grains 9–10, 11, 12
  competitive world markets
    15, 18
  GE food grains 20, 128–30,
    131, 133, 134, 157
  support for supply
    management policies 17–18,
    73
  see also under individual grains
food regimes
  definition and scope 25
  influence and long reach 27
  national regulation 25, 26
  patterns of trade 25–6
  role of grains in formation of
    30–2
  see also British food regime;
    US food regime
food riots 5, 6, 80, 81, 88–9
food security/insecurity 2, 20,
    27, 81
  accessibility to food 83, 88,
    93, 104

food security/insecurity (*cont.*)
   agricultural exports and 93–7
   contributory factors 83–4
   FAO definition 83
   geopolitics of grains and
      93–105
   land expropriation and 153
   land grabs and 150–1
   land reform and 153
   market policies, impact of
      93–100, 105
   measures of 83
   see also world hunger; *and
      under individual nations*
food sovereignty 137
Ford Foundation 43
foreign investment capital 56
Formosa, rice production 39
France
   export subsidies 67
   GE grain production 126
   rice imports 130
   supply management 29, 37
   tariffs 30
   wheat exports 45
   wheat production 32, 65
free trade agreements 26, 58,
      60, 147
   see also North American Free
      Trade Agreement (NAFTA)
free trade basis of British food
      regime 22, 26, 29, 30–1, 86,
      87, 140, 142, 151

G23 72
General Agreement on Tariffs
      and Trade (GATT) 20, 40
   Blair House Accord 70
   and creation of WTO 70
   incorporation of agriculture
      58, 59–60, 62, 68–72
   Most Favored Nation (MFN)
      status 40

and spread of supply
      management policies 40,
      41, 46
   and the spread of the US food
      regime 40
   tariffs, prohibition of 41
   Uruguay Round 59, 62,
      69–70
Genetically Engineered Food
      Alert (GEFA) 107
genetically engineered (GE)
      grains 2, 19, 20–1, 107–34
   adoption and acceptance of
      117–23, 128
   benefits for agrifood
      corporations 119–20, 123–4
   benefits for farmers 118–19,
      121, 123
   Bt crops 107, 111, 113–14, 118,
      129
   crop yields 122–3
   "crop-pulls" 126
   entry into the food system 108,
      112, 113, 126–7, 130
   feed grains 20, 112, 128, 131,
      134, 135, 157
   first generation GE crops 110,
      111, 118, 120, 123
   food grains 20, 128–30, 131,
      133, 134, 157
   global spread of 112–13
   herbicide tolerance 110, 111,
      118, 121, 122
   lack of diversity among 111–12,
      117
   patents and intellectual
      property issues 119–20, 121,
      128–9, 132
   pest management problems
      122
   political-economic factors 128
   process 109–10
   profitability 117

resistance to 20, 107, 120,
    123–30, 131, 133
second generation GE crops
    110
seed market 115, 117, 121, 127,
    157
third generation GE crops 110
    in the world economy 131–4
geography of grain production
    and trade 12–15
geopolitics of grains 2–8, 154–60
    geography of grain production
        12–15
    international grain trade 13–14
    and land reform and
        expropriation 21, 151–4
    role in hunger and food
        security 20, 81–2, 84–106,
        156
Germany
    CAP subsidies 67–8
    land reform 145
    quinoa imports 99
    tariffs 30
Glencore Xtrata 7
global circulation of grains 13–14
global food crisis (2007–8) 12,
    20, 81, 82, 88–93, 105, 156
    biofuel production and 91,
        92
    end of supply management
        and 92–3
    expansion of liberalization and
        92, 93
    export restrictions and 89–90,
        92
    FAO estimates of numbers of
        hungry people 88
    financialization of agriculture
        and 91–2
Global Hunger Index (GHI) 83
gluten-free products 2
Golden Rice 128–9, 133

grains
    annual world production of
        3–4, 3
    cultural importance 3
    differences in grains 8–18
    economic well-being and 2–3
    expansion in grain production
        32
    grain prices 36, 67, 81, 89
    political stability and 2
    predominance of maize, rice,
        and wheat 4, 5
    reserves, elimination of 87, 97
    resource consumption 101
    role in formation of food
        regimes 30
    search for new markets 45, 54,
        62–79, 131, 136
    see also individual grains
Great Depression 28, 33, 34, 35,
    37, 39
Green Revolution 43, 61, 93
greenhouse gas emissions 158
Gunther, M. 130

Haiti, food riots 6, 81, 89
Hall, D. 138
Hassad Food 21
health issues 2
Hodge, General John R. 144
hunger see world hunger

imperial preferences trading
    system, British 40–1
India
    beef production and exports
        101–2, 102, 103, 157
    British India 84–8, 105
    dairy industry 102–3
    export restrictions 90, 92
    famines 27, 84, 86, 87–8, 105
    food insecurity 84–5, 86,
        94–5, 101, 103, 104–5, 157

India (*cont.*)
  food riots 80, 81
  G23 member 72
  GE grain production 113
  government food aid 81
  incorporation into the world
    economy 86, 105
  maize exports 104
  maize production 103–4, *104*
  National Food Security Act
    (2013) 80–1
  rice exports 13, 34, 90, 92,
    95, *95*
  rice production 13
  soybean production 103–4, *104*
  subsistence agriculture 85
  water crisis 103
  wheat exports 85–6, *85*
  wheat production 13, 32
Indochina, rice exports 34
Indonesia
  Cairns Group member 68–9
  food riots 81
  rice production 13
inter-grain competition and
    conflict 8, 49, 50–1, 62–3,
    155–6
  contribution to world hunger
    and food insecurity 84–8,
    105, 135
  economic and political
    divisions 31, 63–79, 135, 152
  global meat production and
    consumption, impact of
    135–6
  search for new markets 62–79
  supply management policies
    and 17–18, 49, 50–1, 73
  wheat subsidy war 63–8
international commodity
    agreements 19, 29, 40,
    42–3, 46, 132
  breakdown of 58, 59

International Dairy Agreement
  64
International Food Policy
  Research Institute (GHI)
  83
International Monetary Fund
  (IMF) 57, 96–7, 147
  structural adjustment loans
  57–8
International Rice Commission
  (IRC) 43, 46
International Rice Research
  Institute (IRRI) 43, 46
International Trade Organization
  (ITO) 42
International Wheat Agreement
  (IWA) 19, 29, 30, 42–3, 45
  breakdown and
    reconfiguration of 58–9,
    62
Italy, land reform 145

Japan
  export subsidies 49
  land reform 145
  per capita rice consumption
    24, 49
  per capita wheat consumption
    24, 49
  price supports 37, 47, 48
  production controls 48
  Rice Control Act 39, 62
  rice exports 49
  rice imports 35
  rice production 34, 35, 39, 47,
    49
  rural radicalism 39
  supply management policies
    29, 35, 37, 47, 60–1, 62
  and tariff reductions 71
  wheat imports 24, 25, 49
Jenkins, C. 93
Jussuame, R. 118

Kinchy, A. 110
Korea
    rice production 35
    see also South Korea
Kraft Foods 107, 127
Kun Hai Lee 72

La Via Campesina 21, 72, 138,
    158
labor exploitation 5
land expropriation 21, 23, 27,
    138–9, 152, 154
    accumulation by dispossession
        141, 150, 151
    colonial 141, 142
    commodification and
        privatization of land 23, 53,
        139, 140, 151
    during British food regime
        140–2, 152, 153
    "land grabs" 21, 147, 150–1
    negative impact on food
        security 153
land reform 23, 137, 139–40,
    142–54
    benefits 145
    demise of 146
    during US food regime 142–6
    market-led agrarian reform
        (MLAR) 146, 147–8, 149,
        154
    neoliberal era 146–54
    positive impacts on food
        security 153
    redistribution of land 139, 140,
        143, 147, 148
    state role 140
land set-asides 70, 71
land tenure 5, 21
    access to land 23, 138, 139,
        140, 141, 151
    communal land 53, 139
    democratic development and 5

indigenous peoples 52–3,
    138–9, 141, 142–3
    land rights 21, 139
    usufruct rights 139
Land-O-Lakes 115
liberalization in agriculture 42,
    58–62, 131, 156
    market price instability and
        92
    resistance to 71–2, 77, 79
    search for new markets
        62–79
    and world hunger and food
        security 79
    WTO promotion of 42, 70,
        71–2, 131
liberalization in the world
    economy 19, 40, 55–8, 68,
    135
    contribution to world hunger
        and food insecurity 84, 88
    cross-border capital flows 56
    new international divisions of
        labor 55–6
    shift away from fixed
        currencies 55
    split between food and feed
        grains 73
    US championing of 40, 41
    weakening of social
        protections 56
    WTO and 70
Liberty Link 121, 122
Liberty Link Rice 129–30
Limagrain 115
livestock industry *see* feed grains;
    meat production and
    consumption
Louis Dreyfus 6, 7, 21

McNary–Haugen bills 37–8
Madabeef 150–1
Magnan, A. 125

maize
  biofuel production 12, 78–9,
    89, 90
  feed grain 10, 12, 15
  food grain 9–10, 12, 17
  forms of 1, 2, 9
  GE maize 107–8, 109, 111, 112,
    113–14, 118, 120, 122, 124,
    126–7, 129, 154
  geographic roots 21
  lack of international
    commodity agreements 46
  land expropriation and 154
  MLAR and 154
  percent exported of total
    production 14
  prices 5, 36, 88, 91
  proportion circulated through
    international trade 44
  representative organizations
    44
  StarLink maize 107–8, 109
  supply management policies
    17, 30, 44, 60, 73, 155
  top maize exporters 13
  top maize producers 13, 132
  world maize production 3, 4,
    9, 11, 36, 77, 134, 154
Malaysia 68–9
maquiladoras 53
market instability 90, 91, 155,
  158–9
marketing agreements 16, 17
  see also international
    commodity agreements
Marx, Karl 176n114
meat production and
  consumption
  confined animal feeding
    operations (CAFOs) 102,
    103, 105
  fall of communism, impact of
    76–7

global expansion in 20, 50,
  73–5, 74, 75, 100–1, 152, 157
impact on feed grain market
  135–6, 154, 158
income levels and 101
increase in animal size 76
resource consumption 101,
  103, 106
tariffs 31
total animals slaughtered 10,
  75–6, 76
Mexico
  Chiapas rebellion 52–3, 77, 79,
    135, 149
  commodification of land 53,
    141
  ejidos 53, 143, 144, 149
  food riots 6, 81, 88–9
  land reform 142–4, 148–9,
    153
  maize production 13, 17, 44, 53
  Mexican Revolution 143
  migration 158–9
  opposition to NAFTA 60, 158
  subsidies 53
  supply management policies
    17, 44
  Tortilla Riots 6, 88–9
migration, international 158–9
millet 67
  world production of 3, 4
Monsanto 19, 20, 78, 110, 111,
  115, 116, 117, 119, 121–2,
  123–4, 125, 126, 128
Most Favored Nation (MFN)
  trading status 40

National Association of Wheat
  Growers (NAWG) 119
national diets, shifts in 24–5,
  47, 49
national regulation 8, 25, 26
  policy differences 15–18

see also food regimes; supply
  management policies
neoliberalism 52, 136–7
  land reforms and 146–54
  see also General Agreement on
    Tariffs and Trade (GATT);
    liberalization in agriculture;
    liberalization in the world
    economy; North American
    Free Trade Agreement
    (NAFTA)
New Deal 38, 39
new international divisions of
    labor 55–6
New Zealand 68–9
Nicaragua, land reform 145
Noble Group 7
North American Free Trade
    Agreement (NAFTA) 60,
    158
  neoliberal policies 52, 131
  opposition to 53, 60, 77,
    149

oats
  feed grain 10
  world production of 3, 4
oil crisis (1973) 57
Olam 7
Organization of Rice Exporting
    Countries 90

Paarlberg, R. 123, 129
Pakistan
  Cairns Group member
    68–9
  food riots 81
  hunger and food insecurity 88,
    94–5, 96–7, 157
  rice exports 13, 95, 95, 96
  wheat exports 95, 96–7
Panama, land reform 145
papaya 111, 114

patents and intellectual property
    issues 119–20, 121, 128–9,
    132
peasant movements 21, 52–3, 72,
    126, 137, 138, 143–4
Peru
  Cairns Group member 68–9
  food security 98
  land reform 145
  quinoa production 99, 100
Philippines
  Cairns Group member
    68–9
  Comprehensive Agrarian
    Reform Program (CARP)
    148
  GE grain production 129
  land reform 148
  rice production 35, 43
Pioneer HiBreed 116
plantation systems 27
Poland, meat production 77
Polanyi, Karl 22, 87
political instability 5, 6, 88
  see also food riots
poplar 114
Portugal 113
price supports 16, 18, 29, 38, 39,
    47, 48, 70
  and artificially high prices 50
  farming income and 47, 48
  function 29
  shaping of farmers' economic
    interests 16
  see also under individual nations
prices
  instability 31–2, 36, 37, 91, 92,
    156
  international commodity
    agreements 19, 29, 40,
    42–3, 46, 132
  regulation of *see* price supports
  see also under individual grains

processed foods 1, 9–10, 11, 12,
    131
production controls 16–17, 29
    function 29
    grain reserves, creation of 17
    land use restrictions and 16,
        48
    marketing agreements 16, 17
production quotas 70
protectionism 6, 14, 27, 39, 50
    see also price supports;
        subsidies; tariffs
public debt, expansion in 57

quinoa 97–100
    food security, impact on 98–9
    prices 100, 100
    production 20, 98–9, 99
    superfood 98

railroad development 86
recessions, global 57
    see also Great Depression
Rhee, Synghman 144
rice
    colonization and 34–5
    food grain 9, 12
    forms of 1
    GE rice 128–30, 133
    geographic roots 21
    Golden Rice 128–9, 133
    international organizations 43,
        46, 90
    lack of international
        commodity agreements 46
    percent exported of total
        production 14
    prices 5, 36, 88, 90
    proportion circulated through
        international trade 44, 46
    supply management policies
        30, 73
    top rice exporters 13

    top rice importers 13
    top rice producers 13
    world rice production 3, 4, 11,
        34–5, 77, 89–90, 134
    see also under individual nations
Rockefeller Foundation 43
Romania
    GE grain production 113
    meat production 77
Roosevelt, Franklin 38
Roundup 111, 117, 119, 121, 122
Roundup Ready wheat 119
Russia
    maize production 36
    wheat exports 13–14
    wheat production 13, 32
    see also Soviet Union
rye, world production of 3, 4

Saskatchewan Organic
    Directorate (SOD) 125
Saudi Arabia
    "land grabs" 150
    price supports 61
    wheat production 61
Scanlan, S. 93
"Scramble for Africa" 141
search for new markets 54,
    62–79, 131, 136
seed industry 5, 19, 132
    commodification of seeds
        119
    GE seeds 115, 119, 121, 127,
        157
    seed saving, prohibition of
        119, 121–2
Sementes Agroceres 116
Senegal, food riots 81
Slovakia 113
Smithfield Farms 77
Smithsonian Agreement (1973)
    55
social support programs 56

sorghum
  feed grain 10
  world production of 3, 4
South Africa
  Cairns Group member 68–9
  G23 member 72
  land reform 147–8
South America
  soybean production and
    exports 77–8
  see also individual nations
South Asia
  food insecurity 94–5
  see also individual nations
South Korea
  land reform 144
  opposition to AoA 72
  rice production 61, 144
  supply management policies
    47–8, 61
  wheat imports 49
Soviet Union
  wheat exports 45
  wheat imports 56
  wheat production 33
  see also Russia
soybeans 10–12
  feed grain 10, 11–12, 15
  food grain 11
  GE soybeans 109, 111, 112, 118,
    122, 124
  geographic roots 21
  percent exported of total
    production 14
  RR soybeans 122
  supply management policies
    155
  top soybean exporters 13
  top soybean producers 13, 132
  world soybean production
    10–11, 11, 77, 134
  see also under individual nations
Spain 113, 114

squashes 111
StarLink maize 107–8, 109, 120,
  126–7
structural adjustment loans
  57–8
subsidies *see* export subsidies;
  price supports
subsistence agriculture 53, 85
sugar beets 111
supply management policies 16,
  32, 34, 37, 39
  feed grain producers and 17,
    18, 50–1, 73
  food grain producers and
    17–18, 73
  GATT and 40, 46
  retrenchment 60, 61, 62, 157
  spread and solidification of 40,
    42, 46, 47, 49, 50, 142
  surpluses, tendency to lead
    to 48
  see also export subsidies;
    price supports; production
    controls; *and under*
    individual nations
surpluses 36, 37, 38, 39, 47, 49
  export subsidies and 47, 50,
    65–6
  production controls and 17
  supply management policy
    and 48
sweet peppers 114
Syngenta 20, 115, 127, 129

Taiwan
  land reform 145
  rice production 35, 47–8
  supply management 47–8
tariffs 14, 30, 37, 50
  AoA tariff reductions 71
  Cairns Group opposition to 69
  GATT prohibition of 41
Terra Firma Capital 21

Thailand
  Cairns Group member 68–9
  land reform 146
  rice exports 13, 34, 46, 90
  rice production 35
  stagnating rural economy 35
Timmer, C.P. 89
tomatoes 110-11, 114, 172n75
Toor, S. 96
trade barriers *see* protectionism
trade unions 56
trade wars 5, 20
  see also wheat subsidy war
Tunisia, food riots 6, 89

ubiquity of grains 1–2
Ukraine
  maize exports 13
  wheat exports 13–14
United Nations 43
  Food and Agricultural
    Organization (FAO) 10, 59,
    81, 82, 83, 88
  Millennium Development
    Goals 81, 83
Uruguay 68
US
  Agricultural Adjustment Act
    (1933) 38
  Agricultural Trade
    Development and
    Assistance Act (1954) 25
  biofuel production 90, 92
  Department of Agriculture
    (USDA) 108
  economic hegemony 26, 29,
    54, 57, 58
  Energy Independence and
    Security Act (2007) 90
  Environmental Protection
    Agency (USEPA) 107, 122
  Export Enhancement Program
    (EEP) 66

  Federal Agriculture
    Improvement and Reform
    Act (1996) 61
  and GATT 40, 41, 69
  GE grain production 111, 112,
    113, *113*, 117–19, 120, 123,
    124, 128, 130, 132, 133
  grain prices 36
  International Wheat
    Agreement (IWA) 43,
    58–9
  McNary–Haugen bills 37–8
  maize exports 13, 14–15, 36, 45,
    108, 132, 133
  maize production 10, 13, 14,
    36, 44, 48, 50–1, 78, 124,
    152
  and NAFTA 53, 60
  New Deal 38, 39
  quinoa imports 99
  rice exports 13
  rice production 61
  shift away from fixed currency
    55
  soybean exports 13, 14, 15, 45,
    132, 133
  soybean production 13, 14,
    50–1, 124
  and tariff reductions 71
  wheat exports 13–14, 17, 45,
    49, 64, 65, 66, 133
  wheat production 13, 32, 33, 34,
    48, 60, 152
  wheat subsidy war 63–8, 69,
    72, 79, 135
US food regime 24–51
  centrality of wheat 151, 152
  contradictions in 50
  cooperation and coordination
    basis 50
  decline of 19, 54, 68, 73, 131,
    146, 152, 155, 156
  effects of 47–51

export subsidies 17, 28, 29, 47,
        49, 50
    international commodity
        agreements 19, 29, 42–3
    and land reform 142–6, 151
    national regulation 22, 27,
        28–9
    origins 31–40
    price supports 28, 29, 38, 60
    production controls 28, 29, 38,
        48, 51, 60, 61, 92–3
    spread of 40–6, 47
    supply management policies
        16, 19, 28–9, 32, 37, 38, 41,
        46, 47, 60, 61, 73, 131, 142,
        152, 155, 156
    surpluses 48
    tariffs 30
Uzbekistan, food riots 81

Venezuela, land reform 145
Vietnam
    export restrictions 90, 92
    rice exports 13, 90, 92
    rice production 13
Vietnam War 57

welfare state contraction 56
wheat
    centrality to British and US
        food regimes 151
    competitive world market 8,
        14, 45, 46
    food grain 9, 12
    forms of 1
    GE wheat 118–19, 125, 126,
        133
    geographic roots 21–2
    international commodity
        agreements 29–30, 42–3
    percent exported of total
        production 14
    prices 5, 36, 57, 67, 88

proportion circulated through
        international trade 44
    Roundup Ready wheat 119
    top wheat exporters 13–14
    top wheat producers 13
    world wheat exports 66
    world wheat production 3, 4,
        11, 33–4, 33, 77, 134
    see also under individual nations
wheat subsidy war 63–8, 69, 72,
        79, 135
Wilmar 7
World Bank 57, 96–7, 103, 147
    and land reform 148
world economy, shift in 54–8
    see also liberalization in the
        world economy
World Food Summit (1996) 81,
        83
world hunger 6, 81
    biofuels production and 90–1
    child hunger 93
    contributory factors 83–4
    famines 20, 27, 84, 86, 87,
        105, 169n56
    food riots 5, 6, 80, 81, 88–9
    land reform and 153
    market policies, impact of
        84–8, 89
    measures of 82–3
    periodic global food crises
        89, 93
    see also food security/
        insecurity; global food crisis
        (2007–8)
world population growth 20, 74
world system theory 163n9
World Trade Organization
        (WTO) 19, 42, 58, 120, 132,
        147
    Agreement on Agriculture
        (AoA) 62, 70–2
    creation of 70

World Trade Organization
    (WTO) (*cont.*)
  and liberalization in
    agriculture 42, 70, 71–2, 131
  and liberalization of the world
    economy 70
  TRIPS 132

Xi JinPing 114

Yemen, food riots 81

Zapatista Army of National
    Liberation (EZLN) 52–3,
    136